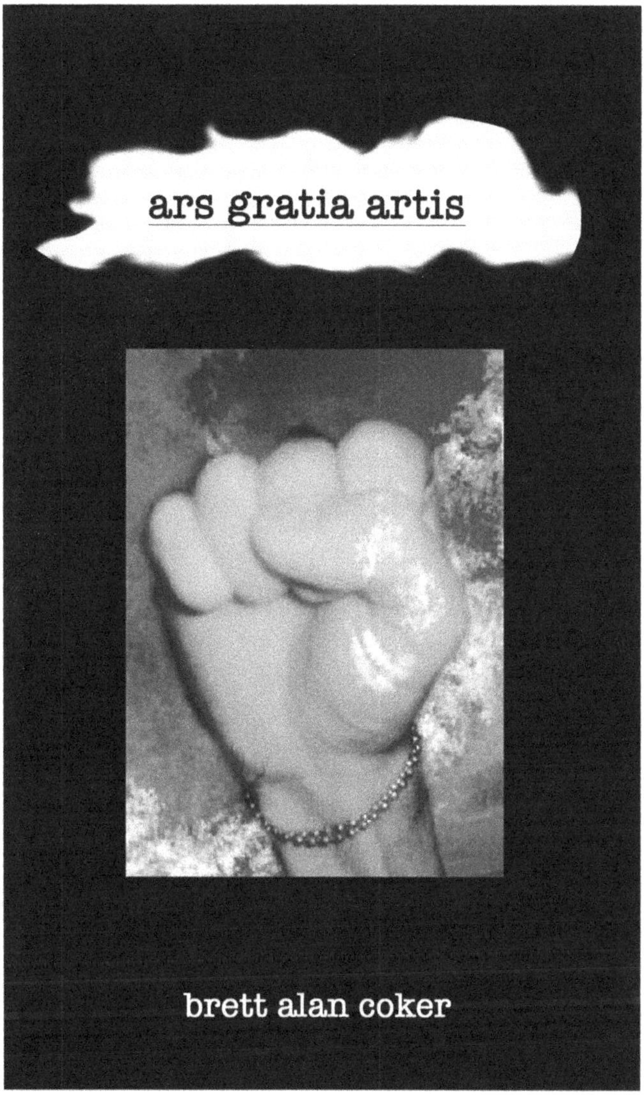

(Original Cover)

ars gratia artis

Brett Alan Coker

A
T.uesday's L.ife B.ooks
inspiration

<u>Series One - Book Three of Nine</u>

ars gratia artis

(- September 18th, 2003 - May 7th, 2004 -)

Original Cover Design - Eric Mackey
Back Photo - Shala Anne Owen

© 2004 Brett Alan Coker
ISBN 979-8-89379-377-2

dedicated to:

_____
(your name here)

.foreword.

i broke this book into three parts. i do not know why. i look at this book as if it were the third part of a trilogy. beginning with <u>'til the streetlights came on</u>, continuing with <u>understanding thursday</u> and now the book that lies before you. being a film buff i know the rules of a trilogy. you continue with the same main characters and add new stuff. but you also go back and visit the places you've been. at the end of the first two parts of this book you will find pieces that are titled after my first two books, stated above. these pieces are merely a collage of lines taken from every poem in each book.

when i began this book, much like with <u>understanding thursday</u>, i had an end in mind. once the actual book i was writing in was full, the book is complete. i began this book in september of 2003. i thought it would take a lot longer to finish it, but i was wrong. <u>'til the streetlights came on</u> was written over a period of four years, and <u>understanding thursday</u> was written in just under two years. i am quite surprised that this book was written in less than one year. and even more surprised at the fact that the pieces included in this book are as good as they are, in their own way. or so i believe.

<u>'til the streetlights came on</u> was a book written by an insecure, depressed teenage boy. <u>understanding thursday</u> was written by a insecure, hurt, and bound-on-revenge quasi-man. <u>ars gratia artis</u> was written by a secure, but sad man. a man who knows that the final rule of a trilogy is that from now on there are no rules and all bets are off.
      i know that from now on, the years after <u>ars gratia artis</u> and this trilogy, my work is going to be a lot different. less personal, perhaps, more open. but like always i don't know what the future holds. and as i step into this next stage of life, with a fresh book in hand, i am curious as to what will come out of me. and anxious to see if i even have another book in me.

- after a name indicates that it has been changed.
* after a title indicates it is lifted from another source.

In order to conserve space and keep these books as inexpensive as possible I have allowed - when applicable - for multiple complete poems to be on a single page.

ars gratia artis

part one

an empty book.
the beginning of a journey.
a pen set to paper.
love in the heart.
head in the clouds.

shadow war

bullets fly
        angels in the night
frightened faces
        scream in the ears
        of the saints

shattered windows
        splintered wood
the good children
        cover their eyes
        bloody tears fall

cemetery gates squeak
the corpses stand
        and dust themselves off
scraping the dirt from their headstones
        never again will they be alone

stone faces bleed
marble statues fall
bronze cherubs melt
        exposing what's inside
dead flesh peeling off
severed limbs stacked in piles

the lady in white gathers her babies
they stare at her
        jewel in hand
she takes them through a garden path
        into the darker realm

deconstruction of a nation

antelopes do not screw for promotions
bats do not kill for pleasure
chimps do not slap their children
    for being too loud
dingoes do not commit murder for shoes
eels do not rape their children
frogs do not ignore life through alcohol
gazelles do not slaughter each other over religion
horses do not beat each other up over women
iguanas do not slit throats because of race
jackrabbits do not inject chemicals for pleasure
kangaroos do not go to war for oil
lambs do not fuck for money
mice do not cut wrists over cheating lovers
narwhals do not stab kids at school
opahs do not send their kids to war
    for false pride
pronghorns do not steal as a hobby
quetzals do not spend their life
    dwelling over money
rheas do not cut each other up
    put the bodies in barrels
    and dip them in acid
swordfish do not snap, shoot coworkers,
    and then blow their own brains out
tapirs do not shoot each other for speaking differently
unicorns do not exist so move on to "v"
    (a little comic levity is always good)
vinegarroons do not ax their wife and kids on christmas morning
warthogs do not beat their wives
    and call them "whores"
x ... um ... fuck
yellow jackets do not disown their homosexual kin
zebras do not hate their own species

it would be nice to be a zebra

quotidian tearjerker: part one

light spills through the shades
        onto her cold naked body
        her arm twitches
        she can't blink
she said "yes" to a ride
        and "yes" to a drink
        and she is positive she said "no"
        when it mattered
but he continued to touch her
        "no" she said
        "i'm not ready"
she knows that she told him "no"
why did he continue?
does he not know the rules?
she has been in the position before
and has told other men "no"
        when the groping goes too far
and they would just stop
        hold her
        and kiss her
why did he keep going?

he kept touching her
putting his body on hers
using his weight to hold her down
grabbing her wrists and pinning them to the floor
        "what is happening to me?" she thought
        "is this real? am i awake?"
        "is this my life?"
she tried to push him off
and he cracked her in the jaw with his fist
        & called her a "fucking bitch!"
put his knee on her thigh
and pushed down hard
smacked her in the mouth
and rammed his tongue down her throat
        "i said 'no'!" she yelled
        "i know i said 'no'" she thought to herself

she has known him for ten years
went to grammar school with his sister
he baby-sat for her neighbors

he ripped off her shirt
and punched her in the stomach
she did say "no", right?
don't people know the rules?
don't men know how to act anymore?

she had bought a new dress for their date
and went to have her hair specially done
this morning she awoke
        and smiled so bright and wide
dying for the hours to pass
        so she could see him
now she watches him walk out of her room
        his pants unbuckled
        panting like a rabid animal
she is sweating
and the blood flows rapidly through her veins
but she feels frozen
        "i am a good person" she thinks
        "this cannot be real"
        "this did not just happen"
she cries
the tears fall onto the blood-soaked sheets
        "what did i do?"
        "what is wrong with me?"
        "why did i deserve this?"

she can feel his seed dripping out of her
and it is all she can feel
she convulses and tucks into a ball
        and vomits on her pillow
        "this cannot be my life"
        "this does not happen to people like me"
        "what is wrong with me?"

the taste of blood is still in her mouth
her left eye is swollen shut
her heart still beats
        although she feels dead inside
she'll have to face him again
she cannot tell anyone
she has to let it go
and accept what happened

"it's not his fault"
"i must have done something wrong"
"i had this coming"

she doesn't know it yet
but his seed inside of her
      will grow
what can she do?
where will she go?

... to be continued ...

from decepticons to the aqua teen

when the revolution comes
    we will have the world in our hands
when the revolution comes
    we will stop to see what we are
when the revolution comes
    we will have the politicians
    on their knees
    like ten-cent whores
when the revolution comes
    the sheep will be slaughtered
    and the lambs will lose their heads
when the revolution comes
    you will know all of your relatives' names
    and forget the names of game show contestants
when the revolution comes
    money will be taboo
when the revolution comes
    the quiet ones will speak their minds
when the revolution comes
    the meek will rise
    the strong will fall
when the revolution comes
    you will survive on minimum wage
    and not have to pay for health care
when the revolution comes
    we will all be one race
when the revolution comes
    class systems will be removed
    hierarchies destroyed
when the revolution comes
    pride will come from creation
    dignity not gained from destruction
when the revolution comes
    we will all be able to breathe
when the revolution comes
    we will all control our destiny
when the revolution comes
    i will be too old to fight alongside it

when the revolution comes

beyond the wire above the ground

black radial scars on the pavement
grill impressions in the dirt
head lights spraying
    into the black of the sky
screams vibrating telephone wire
air-conditioned brain waves
    interfering radio station buzz
seat belts ripping in time
    with the pistons turning
sparks flashing
rain falling
dashboard crumbling
body collapsing over steering wheel
praying to the windshield
confessing to the rearview
spider-cracking paint
shining fragments
eyes twinkling from the blood
glass imbedded in forearm
heart beating in time
    with the keys
        swinging on their ring
rain water purification
blessing the dripping fuel
innocence exploding with the airbag
fear making the temperature rise
our lives turning
a live transmission
dark eyes with pupils shrunk
tail lights flashing
passersby stop and stare
a time of your life
    coming to a close
an autobiography written
    on leather seats with fingernails
circuitry frying
computer shorting out
face swelling with rushing blood

one year later
    the road is still straight
    and bearings intact

a visually exuberant ...

gonna face tomorrow without you (giving up)
    arms falling to my side
to bide my time 'cause you are not (living up)
    to what we had agreed
light a smoke, listen up
    to what i have inside
sit right there, take a drag
    and all of this in stride

even the great movies have sad endings
and bad ones have good themes
the saddest songs are sung with love
to raise emotions high above
the expectations and adroit alliterations
    with alterations at the seams
to cause altercations between the speakers
    high up in the beams
decibels vibrating catwalks
lyrics stalk the audience like prey

gonna face tomorrow without you (giving up)
    arms falling to my side
to bide my time 'cause you are not (living up)
    to what we had agreed
light a smoke, listen up
    to what i have inside
sit right there, take a drag
    and all of this in stride

sob stories are what you remember
when wanting nothing but to cry
yet why do we always smile
when the ugly duckling gets the guy?
try this in this world, this life
    and one thing will be clear
i'm the white knight and you're the duckling
    something i won't go near
your personality is a poison
this lesson you must learn
you still must earn what you want
don't flaunt your pain for sympathy
my love is not for the taking

up on stage in a lonely spot light
        sweat pouring down my face
i set my gauge to rage this night
        space is what i want to take

gonna face tomorrow without you (giving up)
        arms falling to my side
to bide my time 'cause you are not (living up)
        to what we had agreed
light a smoke, listen up
        to what i have inside
sit right there, take a drag
        and all of this in stride

september 24th, 2003 - wednesday

orion is out in the south-eastern sky tonight
looking up at his belt makes me feel
      like a god looking down at the pyramids
basking in creation

untitled and unfinished

the water is growing colder
and rushing away from me
is that a trick you taught it?
it seems that it would be

the water is growing colder
and rushing away from me
it seems to be a trick you taught it
"it's not" you say, let's just wait and see

the water is growing colder
and rushing away from me
is that a trick you taught it?
it seems that it would be
you were always good at hurting
so try your hand at setting free

as i sing this song
i've fooled them all
but the truth makes blind eyes see
as you know these words aren't about you
they simply summarize me

cry, the beloved country *

3:31 p.m.
october 17th
partly cloudy
        chance of rain
a middle-class suburb
the houses are quiet
        birds chirp
bikes sprawled out on driveways
skateboards tossed in the bushes
roller blades sitting on the porch
        the televisions are off
        playstation controllers on the floor
        cell phones on their chargers
        unplugged from the wall
beds neatly made
homework done

one hundred children stand in the street
hand in hand in hand
blue jeans on
        tags ripped off
white tees on
        tags ripped out
look up at the spying sun
black skin melts to brown
brown melts to yellow
yellow to red to white
        to pure
a rainbow of culture
hand in hand they chant
        "cry ... "
they breathe in unison and sway left to right
        "cry ... "
        "cry ... "
hearts beat to the wings of a sparrow
bodies sway to the tune of the leaves
        "cry ... "
eyes widen as they smile
some squint as they laugh and chant
        "cry ... "
for the beauty of the sunrise
        "cry ... "

for the sound of a lover's laugh
    "cry ... "
for the baby in the womb
    whose mother will not make it
    "cry ... "
for the daughter to a fallen father
    "cry ... "
for the son of a killer
    who will never live down his heritage
    "cry ... "
for the boy with the most important
    novel of the century
    in his head but will snort it away
    "cry ... "
for the mother whose children were murdered
    while playing in the yard
    "cry ... "
for the starving refugees
    with distended bellies and bulging eyes
    "cry ... "

the children close in to form a circle
connect to become whole
dropping to their knees
laying their heads and hands on the asphalt

"cry ... "
"cry ... "
"cry ... "

no name #6 (missed misery) *

for Elliott Smith

just one more song before the bars close
just one more please before you go
another encore is all we want
        then you can hit the road
we have driven all night to see you
        to watch you and hear you sing
i can't bring myself to cry before strangers
but that's what your words do to me
cigarettes burn all around
        this club is full of smoke
drinks are pouring
        voices laughing
but i am lost inside your voice
to me it feels like we are all alone
        you   me   your music
together forever more
wondering now if you knew then
that headlines would soon read "dead at 34"

'last call' was yelled and you did 'say yes'
        to one final round
bound and determined to destroy yourself
        right before our eyes
placating us with your "i'm okay"
you were telling 'the biggest lie'
looking for an ease to your suffering
like a 'needle in the hay'
like a 'roman candle' you were 'good to go'
but only to 'bottle up and explode'

we're never gonna know you now
but we're gonna love you anyhow
we're never gonna know you now
but we're gonna love you anyhow

you packed up your cases and put them in the van
ran your hand through your hair and looked down the road
staring into the darkness before you
you shook my hand and said "good-bye"
becoming another "no name"

like all the others you meet on the road
in every city   in every bar
          you mustn't look too far to find us
          the ones who look at you with love
i looked forward to your next visit
          to our small town
another show, song, and shared word
i remember you driving away that night
tail lights disappearing through a turn
and when i learned of what happened not long after
i cried because i felt i should
          but still
i just wanted one more encore
one more song
and a chance to say good-bye
now i know i never will

we're never gonna know you now
but we're gonna love you anyhow
we're never gonna know you now
but we're gonna love you anyhow

you said 'everybody cares. everybody understands'
but 'i didn't understand.' and i still don't.

we're never gonna know you now
but we're gonna love you anyhow
we're never gonna know you now
but we're gonna love you anyhow

haddonfield*

a world away from my home
friends are left behind
alone in a sea of new faces
i feel alone   i miss them all
this   i know
       is just a taste of the future
the names i know
       and the faces that go with them
       will be forgotten someday
it's strange to look around and recognize nothing
to breathe air (smog)
       from a land 1,000 miles away

why am i here?
what am i doing?
is there a purpose?
to visit places in a movie
a piece of art that means so much to me
but doesn't mean a thing to many others
all around are people who love what i love
research and watch the same things i do

celebrities are everywhere
celebrated by true fans
unknowns to the majority
most of them make livings from conventions
admired and adored for something they did
       20 years ago
and either never seen since
       or not too successful
most of these people
       are the foundations for films today
all those shitty teen slasher pictures
       of the 90's and now
are based on the unknowns of the 70's

a girl i saw in a movie back in 1988
       is in a room upstairs
i was 7 and she is the only one of my childhood crushes
       that still burns today
meeting her was enchanting
       but like all things

          it took away the fantasy
she once was a smiling face on a screen
          completely unattainable
now she is here in person
and she is just what she is
          a person

i have dreamt about coming here for years
          seeing the sights and sites
          the people and persons
i'm finally living that dream
i've been to those places
          immortalized in film
and burnt into my memory
i've lived my dream
now what can i do
          with the rest of my life?

overheard in california
one black girl speaking to another: "... fucked andré."
woman on phone: " (crying) i just want to get away from you."
indigent men: "hey, can you help us out?"
wreaking of b.o. guy: "do you know where i can score some marijuana?"

vincent's drug*
on a downtown street today
a man sat tapping his foot
to the rhythm of a band in his head
bottle in hand and he was daydreaming
        on a steaming manhole cover
droopy red eyes with a jagged smile
        from a bar room brawl
nose like a button-hook pattern
        crooked from the get-go
scars on his forehead from cracked tiles
        in a bathroom stall

but he wasn't a failure
        raising kids in these fucked-up times
who went on to prosperity
        as he jagged smiled and stood in line
for food stamps and handouts
        nodding his head to that 3/4 time

abused as a child, wild as a teen
learning the hard way, making parents scream
seeing the smile of his new born babe
set off the alarm that it's time to be a dad
turned in his keys to the kingdom
for a 9 to 5 and little league team

needing that fix of happiness
to make it go away
no 401(k) or any use for a three-piece
just smiles from his children and he's good to go

november 12th, 2003 - wednesday

august 2003, Jonah is singing about
    those seashell hips
i don't know where you are or who you're with
i'm positive though that my name has forgot your lips

shiznatis

i had a little drink and lied about it
so what i'm just hurting myself
at least what i put in my mouth
wasn't a part of someone else
so you found the bottles
i barely tried to hide
who cares?
you gave it away to that frat fuck
because you say you're lost inside
pretend to care about me
then spread for the next hard cock
blaming it all on me makes it easier
    for you to take that walk

the day the rain falls
    unfinished

when the colors run from your face
it's an everyday displacement
of the energy you have inside
so don't hide, just abide
the lines i'm about to send
it'll take time but we'll be in love again
and forget whether this is
the beginning or the end

will you let me be great for you?

untitled

sister samantha with trees dying in your yard
sister samantha why do you find life so hard?
sister samantha leaves piled against your fence
sister samantha are drugs your only defense?

quarter-bag brothers with those dime-store clothes
foes around the corner don't dare leave the house

don't give it up for a powder in a bag
there is more in life for you to grab
you're a fool but i still want you
and i'm stupid for giving you a chance

concert girl
(or "the one who knows everyone but always ends up alone")

standing in the crowd with your o.d. satchel
covered in band buttons
here for the opener and not the headliners
making eyes at the singer
hoping he'll remember
last fall in bed with The Early November
flashing your goods to Celebrity
and tossing off Acceptance
lovin' up to Jonah
tryin' to fellate his microphone-ah

november 26th, 2003 - wednesday

that fake smile has been on your face for so long
it's like it's almost real
at least my eyes are so used to it
that you can no longer steal
        the hope inside my heart

ra.ho.wa*

where did it go
that time in our lives
when we were all the same?
just smiling faces sharing a world
laughing eyes and golden days
how did we generate this hate?
we are all in this together
leading the same lives
this degradation needs to stop
stop the hatred of a color
forget your peeves with a belief
this all needs to stop
clasp hands and see that inside
      our hearts all beat
        to the same rhythm of the night
stop the fighting over holy land
stop fighting over the right to breathe
all of the ground we walk on should be shared
no one should be told to leave because of a skin tone
      or sexual preference
we are all in this together
this all needs to stop
this hate we have in our minds
where did it go
the time in our lives
when we were all the same?
just smiling faces sharing a world
laughing eyes and golden days
how did we generate this hate?

jacky d. & o.j.

as kids we would sit around and dream
about the great things we were gonna do

as teens we planned to do these great things
but ended up just sitting around

as men we sit around and try to remember
what those dreams once were

jag ar nyfiken*

i was never the kind of kid to believe
in everything my parents and teachers said
i'm not a 9-to-5 guy
with a wife and two kids in the suburbs
i just can not take what people say is the truth
        as the truth

i have to wake up hung-over with a pounding headache
        pussy on my breath
some ugly bitch shooting up next to me on the floor
telling me with her black teeth and yellow eyes
        that she was a model once
i have to look around the room at the dozen naked bodies
        of all shapes and sizes
pounding away at each other
        or shaking from an overdose
i have to see the coke and hash on the table
        the crack pipes
        the baggies of junk
the crying girl in the bathroom
        with blood dripping from between her legs
        and a bottle curled in her fist
two week-old make-up streaking her face
        like tears of irony

i have to wake up some day
        and see this
and then finally realize for myself
that this is not how life was meant to be

white socks & the kthomas shirt

in elementary school the pigtailed sweet girls
wanted to kiss the good-looking sweet boys
while the other boys played kickball
and the ugly-duckling girls read

in middle school we became mixed
with all of the other schools from across town
and the pigtailed sweet girls
    wanted to kiss the rebel boys
    with dyed-black hair
    and Marilyn Manson shirts
who smoked cigarettes and weed
    they'd get high together
and some of those girls
    would give up their innocence

some of the good-looking sweet boys
    became popular guys
who began to drink and take advantage
    of the remaining sweet girls
and touch them in places
    they weren't ready to be touched
the other good-looking sweet boys
    became pimply faced and awkward
and could no longer get the pigtailed sweet girls
just the prim and proper pure little daddy's girls
    whom wouldn't kiss or touch at all
the non good-looking boys played sports
the nerds studied
and the ugly ducklings read

in high school the weed smokin' rebels strangely
    were still dating middle school girls
the pigtailed sweet girls
    used and tossed away,
    were handed to the upperclassmen
friends of the pigtailed girls' brothers
the popular good-looking guys now got
    both older and younger girls
drank more and kicked the shit out of the nerds
and the pimply-faced ex good-looking sweet boys

the pimply-faced ex good-looking sweet boys
would get fed up with the non-touching
    non-kissing prude sweet daddy's girls
they'd go for older and hotter girls
    but fail
the prude non-touching daddies' girls would then find
the juniors and the seniors and suddenly
    they were ready to be touched
and the pimply-faced ex good-looking sweet boys would be hurt
having to watch a love they had
    be used and thrown away
the pimply faced ex good-looking sweet boys
    would be alone
and too hurt to notice
    the eyes of the ugly ducklings
looking up from their books
    coveting from afar

(- a few years later -)

the weed smokin' rebels
    were still listening to Marilyn Manson
    dating middle schoolers
    and were the same height as they were four years ago
    and still as smart

the sweet pigtailed girls, now two generations used, are alone because
    their date-rapin' boyfriends
    are playin' ball in college
drinking and cheating
    using all of the un-popped leftovers
the sweet pigtailed girls are now alone
and the pimply-faced ex good-looking sweet boys
    are bigger
    stronger and have cleared-up faces
and no longer care
    about the used pigtailed sweet girls
although some of the sweet boys became hurters
    after being hurt themselves
    most got back on track
the once again good-looking sweet boys
    are now in love
with those ugly ducklings

        now turned beautiful swans
        whom liked to be touched plenty
        and still have their innocence
        plus culture and intellect

the non good-looking boys got scholarships
        will do well in college academically
        and leave sports behind
they'll marry an ugly duckling because of who they are
        and not what they look like
and they will be the happiest of them all

(- to recap -)

those sweet pigtailed girls are used up early
        and look 40 when they're 20
        make-up covering their faces
faces that have been jerked off on one too many times at keggars
because their boyfriends were horny
        and the girls were raggin'
        dark shadows under their cold eyes
dropping out of college to have the jock-stars kids
        ironically they give birth to ugly ducklings
        who will be greater than their parents ever were

the jock-stars were once good-looking sweet boys
        who drank too early
        and fingered the sweet girls
        before they understood their bodies
they used these women because they hated them
possibly because their dad pushed them too hard
        or their mom held them too much
they soon become old men with shot knees
        and bloodshot alcoholic eyes
cold dead eyes like their wives'
        selling cars to those millionaire nerds
        who run their own companies
        set for life and laughing inside
        at the all-star quarterback
        working on commission
it's fine though
        the nerd boys will marry
        many ex-cheerleaders

        turned ex-models turned ex-beautiful
        who will use the nerds for their money
the nerds won't care though
        they did something with their lives

the ugly ducklings become the educated beauties
        the working mothers
        who are the most amazing
all they want is love and to share their love
        with a man and a family

the strong non good-looking guys
        have technical degrees
        become good providers and just want to love
        and be loved
to raise their kids the same
        and they will
to reiterate—
        they will be the happiest of us all

that one kid in the class who wasn't great looking
but not too bad looking either
        who never spoke up but got good grades
        he'll soon be teaching the class
        that you once shared
teaching your kids what you never learned
and he won't be surprised
        when your kids become depressed
because he knows how their parents once were
        and probably still are

some jock-stars will come back and try to teach
        only so they can coach
and try to make friends with the new jockies
        and be a mentor
but ignore the other boys
and make those sweet boys even bigger introverts
        and outsiders
the coaching jock teacher will suck at his job
        just like he sucked off that guy at college
        after one too many beers
        and found he had something to hide
his class will be failing

so he'll change their grades
to make himself look good
i swear this happens
how else would i have passed freshman algebra?

that guy with the camaro
who deflowered your ex girlfriend
and kicked your ass in the parking lot at sonic
will still have that camaro when he is managing that sonic
his daughter will drive that camaro
and your son will be fucking her in the ass
in that camaro in the parking lot of that sonic

those two talented black boys who were the backbone
of the football and basketball teams
who could've been great
will hang with the wrong crowd
and expect to be handed things they didn't earn
spend off-court time smokin' chronic
and will eventually rob a mcdonalds
but be too high to remember where they parked
and will be arrested

that boy who spent countless hours in his garage
working on his car in the cold
drinking to stay warm
will take his first drive
and end up killing his girlfriend's grandparents

that posh uptight rich bitch
who was always too good for everyone
and who kept her virginity
all throughout college
will lose it to a guy ten years older
who has a wife and kids
his wife will find out and divorce him
he'll lose everything he had
and the posh ass bitch will also leave him
he won't be the the last one she does this to

that guy who dated the same girl
all throughout high school and college
who got married and had two great kids

and a beautiful home in suburbia
    will end up being the guy
    from the previous story

the valedictorian will go to harvard law
    marry a less goal-oriented man
    and have a few kids
the dad will raise them while the mother works
by the time the kids go to law school
the letters home will be addressed "dear dad,"
mom will be too busy to read them anyway

the kid who knew all of the answers to all of the questions
    because his mom was a teacher and smothered him in
    knowledge
    and other things
    he'll get perfect scores on the a.c.t. and s.a.t.s
he'll hit the real world
    and see that he's nothing special
    there are a ton of geniuses in the world
he'll realize he never made any friends
    except for his mom
and he'll blow his million dollar brain all over the walls of a $25 motel
    and fall over dead on his princeton
    acceptance letter

the battle scars we receive during these days
    can be worn as badges of honor
    or a crown of thorns

i can not say whether i am right or wrong
    about this formula
    it is a good general idea though
all i can say is what i was
    what i became
    and what i hope to be

i was a good-looking sweet boy who once was a boyfriend
    to the cute pigtailed sweet girls
    the ones who would eventually become
    those used broken angels
i became a pimply-faced awkward boy who raged
    and turned into a muted demon

i was one of the boys who was hurt
        and turned to hurting
        trying to be a popular jock
touching girls before they were ready
        and burning for it to this day
persecuting the nerds
        because i didn't understand them
wanting to be a rebel but didn't have the balls
        and had too much brains
i later became good-looking again
        but still hurt women
        and would use them to make them hurt
except the terrible thing is i never hurt
        the girls that hurt me
most of the girls who hurt me
        become women who hurt themselves
        or marry men to do it for them
i fell in love with an ex ugly duckling
        now turned beautiful swan and hurt her
then i left her and she hurt me
        she found a good-looking sweet boy
who somehow made it
        through this process untouched
        and unchanged and is still
        a good-looking sweet boy
        who deserves who he has
although hurt once more i did not resort to hurting
        and hopefully never will again
i now just want to love and be loved
i was that sweet boy who became a tortured teen
        with a brilliant mind and endless dreams
all i want is to be that sweet boy as a man
        and i'm trying hard to do so

'til the streetlights came on

why can't i wake from this horrific dream?
        suburban kids fight the pain inside
my heart it hurts, my mind it's raped
        so fuck it
dreaming of a better place
        ... and what we can never have again
my emotions i never show
        streams of crimson flow
absolution
        i was just wondering why you hate me?
the day i became a puppet ...
        shut up, that is bullshit!
can i still love her?
        i love fear
i'm taking any and all chances that are thrown at me
        with her beautiful brown hair
... because i'm their fucking floor mat
        i've told you i hate you and called you a bitch
i felt i must do something to fill this void
        i want to go back to playing kickball
someday
        no longer the blood of christ to drink
once again, look at this ass!
        father midnight croons
sees beauty in trivial things
        you wonder what happened to those days of old
as i look upon this boy
        and more to her
 i fucking deserve it
        in a shrill demonic tone
my soul is black like my heart
        i no longer dream
the losing of innocence
        fighting narcotic hordes
        of barbiturate serpents
wonderland is gone
        i conclude that i cannot be free
the last breaths of cursed laments
        ruining it forever
feeling sad & lonely
        eyes glass over in onyx
melts tarry roofs

        in the land of ivory bullets
        with chromium shells
in the zoo inside myself
        its immortality
it shatters my vision
        i choke on my own hate
reaching up to touch the ground
        scribbling down bits of words
in a ruby sky
        i saw a prick
the sins of the past
        my black hell
i am inside you although i hurt you
        cold & crystal
take me back
        it is like i am a pain junkie ...
the sex of summer begins
        a gliding waltz of coital pleasure
long dirty hair hangs ...
        i have you fooled, but cool
the calm before the storm
        putrid soldiers of material things
terror reaffirms its place
        one slip
as i become erect
        a poetic playground
a constant raining of urine
        i follow the blazing star
shedding away inhibitions
        in a numeric system of love
of bubonic decay & pornographic waste
        killing my soul
i serenade with the devil
        blossoming infidelity
a prepared fate
        creeping
ten minutes from now
        in your blaze of glory
the one who sings to her
        i'll still put up with you
be strong i know you can
        but we still play on
love that was so pure

        jade fingerprints not viewable by your ruby eyes
supposedly in a dream world
        an insecure boy
life spins around me
        the image of who i was
dark shots of cynic juice
        the end is near
dreams in the day
        after we destroy you
corrupt you as you did us
        i was a child then ...
become a junky
        with the bang of our gong
        & the rise of the sun
spinning iz my mynd
        raysed it 2 my lips
i no longer feel alone
        slowly & surely
and all i ask is why?
        shit pisses me off
not fit for any love
        sing it soft & slow
it happened on a cold dark night
        scribing a requiem of mortal abortions
your unicorn is that one girl
        a savage world
'til the streetlights came on

part two

facing your past.
another year dies.
wanting to move on.
still scared of tomorrow.
taking a chance anyway.

because you come from the earth*

you know her
in your life you'll know a few just like her
a girl who stands in place to save face
never concede to another when she thinks she's right
she'll hold her own and stand her ground
as long as others are around
but when she gets home
      and feels alone
        that's when it comes
she'll battle you with words all night
and tell you stories that are never about her
a friend, a friend's friend, a cousin
she has none of her own
what is there to tell people
      when you spend your life alone?
too scared to love anyone
      or share what's on her mind
yet the scarred heart she bears
      needs to find
that one person to love her and hold her
and tell her it's all right
when she gets home to a dark room
      a chilly bed
      and the feelings in her head
this is when she breaks alone
her sobbing eyes and pounding chest
      shaking the walls of her room
not worried about waking her parents
the pills they pop will keep them sedated
      'til tomorrow afternoon
she is the kind of girl who lives in her shell
      not because she was hurt and put there
it's just that no one
      helped her out

all you need is that spark
the spark that lights a match
a match that creates a flame
a flame that starts a fire
a fire that burns a heart
a heart that kindles a mind
a mind that gives birth
        to a revolution

all i need is that spark

_____ slunt

what did you mean
when you said "you make me feel like a person?"
you smile at me
and it seems that i make you
        something more than you are
at least these are the lies you expound
vomiting these lies in my face
are you sure it is i who raises your spirits?
what if it is the powder in your nose?
        or your connect-the-dot arms?
or the cum inside you
        that didn't cum from me?

that dried blood around the rim of your nostril
that flakes off into your food
the pus leaking from your abscess

you have become a monster
a chemically-run robot
this is what you are
this is how you choose to be
and you say you are happy
and i am the one who makes you that
therefore i am responsible for your destruction?

the gold band on my finger is a jail sentence
        a sinking weight
the gold is a time-release poison
        to kill me over years

you're weak
which is why you hide in paraphernalia
but i am weaker
        because i let you fall

january 14th, 2004 - wednesday

why is it that most people who believe in god
    don't believe in themselves?
give thanks to him if you must
but take credit for what you create

leaving lenexa

is it time to say good-bye?
is it time to walk away?
i fought and won those battles
i was fighting yesterday

so alone in the house that held me
        and the neighborhood around
there is no one left for me here
        i scream and it makes no sound
doing the same things   repeating
day to day to day
with nothing left to say
adult life is eating
        my childhood away

with aged lines streaking my face
like wood grain on window sills
i must escape this place
life fades as time stands still

no one makes me warm
no one holds me close
no one remembers the good times
no one forgets the bad
doing the same things   repeating
day to day to day

i will never make a difference
        or do anything great
be anyone important
if i stay it will be too late
but i'm so scared to make a change

i have done all i can do here
no more achievements to be made
greatness and glory lie before me
why face the burning sun
        when lying in the shade?

booze & bitterness *
(or "the erosion of manhood")

something happened
something changed
what happened to families?
and committing for life?
where did all of the men go?

everyone is running
they are all scared   afraid
too weak to last

people want love
but when they find it
they want more
from someone else

i've always believed in living for yourself
sometimes though you have to live for others
in the world of yesterday
men and women would marry for life
men would pay attention to their kids
men would be men

this is a different world
different life
a new america
i still dream of a nation
that has a strong family structure

choices   choices
so many choices
a $30,000 sports car
or two kids and a dog
creating is important
just don't ignore your children
to write your shitty novel

where did all of the men go?
where are they hiding?
why are they afraid to be loved?

put down the remote and pick up a fairy tale
       and sing your kids to sleep
take a day off from work
      pack a picnic
        and show your kids the world

where are you hiding?
where did all of the men go?

i won't hide with you
i am not a man yet
but when i am i will earn the right
to be called one

needlepoint in the moonlight
(or "a lesson in addiction")

melting in a spoon
like my heart that melts for you
do it with me and you'll see
so many glorious images
you can taste the air

feel the burn
rushing through your veins
        the infinite orgasm

pierce my skin like a bullet
        and fill me with your liquid love
close your eyes
        feel the world spin around you

sweat at night
        and shiver
the powder screams your name
        heroin/e in distress
wanting to be comforted
        and to comfort you
to grab a hold of your atoms
        pull them and manipulate

i draw pictures on my arms
        to cover your (my) tracks
a silver cross connects the lines
a symbol of salvation
        to mask my damnation

it's okay that you do not love me anymore
so stay with me because you're weak
i have changed i know this
you just can't let go of the image
        of who i once was

you see me
        my destruction
the shell of a body and mind
        and you know i will destroy myself

yet you too continue on
        your habit is also growing
        like your disgust for me
i trapped you and will control you
like the substance does me
you are mine forever

let's begin our fall

... a beautiful world of stars & sighs*
(or "a war with the angels that led to forgiveness")

raise your hand if you have battled god
once again i am the only one to experience this

it began when i was a child
i felt alone like i do now
and people would always talk about faith
        and beliefs
i had neither
i was lost and confused
i was left out
i wasn't a part of anything
so in order to deal with not understanding
i turned to rebelling
i would say i didn't believe
        or that i didn't care
when the truth was that i was ashamed of myself
so i made up for this
by acting like this was my choice

i was so pathetic and weak
i gave in because i was unable to accept
        or just think for myself
i mocked those with faith
because i hurt so much
faking my hatred made me feel strong

i battled god

i still don't trust or believe
        in organized religion
to conform to a set belief structure
would make me have to adhere to rules
        and morals that i don't believe in
i found that in essence you are your own god
i live by rules set forth by
        my own mind
i govern my own decisions
and i punish myself for breaking my own morals

i don't know why everyone is so afraid of their god
when i finally listened to his voice
i felt that all he wants
        is my love and happiness
he doesn't expect me to bow or pray
        or beg for forgiveness
        or live in his debt
he just wants me to live a good life

i battled god

and during that war i saw
        that i was the only one
        turning to hate
i would cuss and yell and scream
and he would just listen
his presence was all he gave
he did not yell back
        or curse me
he just listened

he gave me the choice to acknowledge him or not
and i could have just not acknowledged him
but i chose to acknowledge him
        by fighting him
because i was so afraid to love him

come one day i gave up
something popped inside
a warmth filled me
a smile crossed my face
i looked up and saw him
and opened my heart and mind
        and let his beauty in

it was so extraordinary
i found the strength
        by letting him love me
and i turned to love him
because we are one and the same
we are both in this world
        to be something great

i battled god
        and we both won

and no one can ever
        take that away from me

cigarette burns & emulsion scratches
(or "a changeover to the final reel")

i keep repeating to myself that "it's not over"
that pitiful little bit of faith
keeps me from crying in my sleep
and burning the pictures of us
        and the poems i wrote

(i hurt so much right now
        because this is the first thing
        i've ever written about you
        instead of for you
        and i never wanted this day to come)

take your time and placate me
saying you'll "come back" and
        "we'll be together again"
we both know it won't happen

"the more i let you go,
        the easier it will be
        for you to walk away"

i never thought we'd come to the end
i cannot believe i have known you this long
the story of our love
        and coming to be together
is a story to write about
i just never wanted to scribe the final act

come back to me
you sexy, tattooed
        pierced, little hottie

i know that you are still young
        and you have the right to live
experience your life before you settle down
and just because i'm ready doesn't mean
        you owe me that

i just want to be with you
        for a little while longer

i'm so full of love
        and i just want to share it with you
when i'm alone i begin to rage

i have not felt like this
        since before we were together
and when you kissed me it went away
don't let today be the day i remember
        you leaving and walking away

when angels wish for snow

christmas lights twinkling
    and reflecting in the eyes of a child
whose parents feed him pills instead of hope
video games and toys
    but no love

sleet and frost on the driveway
where he has never played basketball
    although they have a goal
snow and ice in the backyard
    where he has never played catch

the bike he got last year
the expensive one with the donut and pegs
is still in the corner of the garage
they bought it for him
    but didn't teach him to ride

every CD he ever wanted he has
every game he wants is in his room
a room covered in posters and pictures
boxes of comics and cards
worth a fortune
    but isn't worth shit to him

this christmas he didn't make a list
    or ask for a single thing
there are thirty presents under the tree
    and they all have his name

the photo album has dozens of pictures
    from all the holidays past
with him sitting cross-legged on the floor
    swimming in a sea of wrapping paper
he holds his gifts
    and gives a smile
kind of happy
the only time his parents look at him
    and actually see him
is when looking through the viewfinder

he knows his parents are wealthy

        smart and successful
important and well-regarded
flying here and there
        for conventions and meetings

what do you get for the boy
        who has everything?
how about a hug?
        or the time of day?

this year he is making a deal with god
        and santa
        to bring him something great
all he is wanting is someone
        who tells him they love him
        and means it

the suicide society of the summer session *

what am i?
what can i be?
some things i can change
some i can't

what am i?
male   a born kansan   caucasian
a citizen of the u.s. of a.
a life-form on earth
a mammal
these are the things i can't change

what can i be?
if i choose i can be a part of anything
a christian   a catholic   a jew
a buddhist   a baptist   a satanist
an atheist   or agnostic

a democrat   a republican
a liberal   a conservative
        an independent
i can't change the country i was born in
        but i can change in which one
        i live

i could be pro-choice   or pro-life
a homosexual or homophobe
a racist or a fighter for all races
i could be a patriot
        or an anarchist
bourgeois   or a plebeian
there are thousands of organizations
        and brotherhoods and groups
        i could join and subscribe to
the nra   kkk   or aryan nation
hundreds of beliefs to believe in
but the more clubs i join
        the narrower my mind gets
i have to take on their rules
        their mentality
i have to abide by their code of conduct

the more i become part of something
the more i can't think for myself
i'd have to keep up appearances
    to be a member
even if i fully agree with what they teach
the more we judge and categorize each other
    the more we put ourselves at odds

if i were a nazi i'd have to hate you
    if you were a jew
even though you're a good guy
we could grow up next to each other
    and be best friends
but if you signed on to fight
    for a baby's right to life
and i fought the right to choose
    we'd become sworn enemies

can't we just stop subscribing
    to societies that make
    us hate each other?

violin strings & garrote wires
(or "instruments of a bitter end")

you are the corruption
the deception and the lies
surprise surprise
the ties that bind are breaking
you can see it in my dying eyes

so despite the home you gave me
and that little bit of love
i'm leaving you behind me
i know when enough is enough

with your tough-man attitude
and father-figure façade
i have to pretend i like you
and my performance deserves applause
you sit me down and give me rules
to try and teach me how to live
but i'll give you a little
surprise surprise my friend
you have no fucking clue
living in a tiny house with your dogs
      and your cans of brew
killing yourself and blaming the world
with nothing else to do

cuggle
it's not a matter of you being mine
      i'm still your friend
and i want to be there to hold you
         when you cry

discreet lines & downhill eyes
(or "consumption of the jonestown fla-vor-aid")

death makes you famous
    so why are we all afraid to die?
and why do we cry
    for those who go before us?

3,000+ killed in nyc on 9/11
    and we sped into war
as of now we have killed 9000+
    citizens (women & children)
    or what we call "collateral damage"

a young black girl is kidnapped
    raped and sodomized
and it's on the news for a day or two
    and no one is brought to justice
a rich white girl is murdered five years ago
    and the investigation is still open

genocide is committed by the u.s. government
when they slaughter a church in waco
    and the murderers go free

we pay taxes for our big screens & cadillacs
and those taxes pay for bombs
bombs to be dropped on
    children in other countries
it's okay though
    because they have dark skin

we ignore those starving
    and dying in the third world
to watch a fat business man live life
    like one of those kids on an island
they eat bugs everyday
when he does though he wins $1 million
but we'd rather watch him
he'd look better on the cover of 'e.w.'

we'll look past a basketball star
    raping a 15-year-old

and pissing on her
just like we look passed
the 500,000 dead in rwanda in '94

i'm not trying to judge
        or point the finger
because i too am part of the populous
        that is high on apathy
it runs through my veins like $5 coffee

do i give to charities?
        or fight for a cause?
no
i don't
do i give my time?
        or volunteer?
hell no
but i do sit around and complain

all i can say i do
        is think about people whom i don't know
        and will never meet
all i can say i do is learn about
        their tragedy
as i watch a documentary i rented
        which costs more
        than they'll make in a year

i am a no name nobody
a boy you see on the streets
a suburban falsity
a caucasian fraud
i feel for those less fortunate than me
because i have the opportunity and the luxury to
to stop and think about others' lives
out of boredom i learn about their world
i read words that submerge
        my consciousness
        into another realm
i dodge bullets and scrounge up food
        only in my mind
i'm so fat and full of fast food
and i veg while i read about

        you starving savages

i write about you to exploit you
i want to achieve glory
        and attain accolades for my words
words based on your struggle

you are on the brink of death
and i'm on the brink of fame
i'm gonna be rich because you're not
and this is possible
because i'm from
        the u.s. of a.

the 4th reel epiphany
(or "overcoming thinking for yourself")

unnamed terror
an imposing imminent threat
stock up on bottled water, batteries,
        and gas masks
duct tape your windows and doors,
        practice duck & cover
we are at level (agent) orange
protect your kids from zyklon b
by feeding them massive amounts of vitamins
        and strike carbs from their diets
you should be cautious

there is terror all around
it could be in that envelope
        or unmarked package from israel
an imposing imminent threat
we are at level 8-4
        (watch out for bowser!)

be afraid
be so very afraid
do not venture outdoors
do not talk to people on the street
they may exhale mustard gas
or have anthrax in their pores
be afraid

go about your normal lives
but just be
        scared fucking shitless!!
fill up your gas tanks
buy a lot to maintain economical stability
just trust in your government
we know how to waste, er, spend your money

if you see any black males in their 20's
        walking through the suburbs, please
        call the cops immediately
or any middle eastern men in the farmland
        call the a.t.f. and i.n.s.

        and geraldo

everything is fine
nothing to see here
        oh fuck, what was that explosion?!
don't look over there!
keep looking forward
follow the lemming in front of you
put on your running suit and reeboks
pass the collection plate
        then the dirty needle

there is an unnamed terror
terror without a face
it will strike soon
it will strike in enough time
        for me to look good
        come election year

there is not only a threat in your country
        but your city
        your state your 'hood
but also in your computer
the threat is an e-mail
        subject heading: xxx!!

terror in your keyboard
fear is in your breath
terror at your playgrounds
fear inside your kids

i don't think i'm being told the truth
i think someone is lying to me
but i appointed people to think
        and make decisions for me
i'll just stick to fearing and consuming
you just stick
        to slowly killing me

you are what it is i see in you
(you just have to see it in yourself)

she wrote: too often i get scared
and i don't know what to do
i loved you, us, and what we had
i see how sweet you can act
and hear the polished words you say
promising your heart and body
        are only for me
but behind my back you give it away
i don't know what to believe

he wrote: when the colors run from your face
it's an everyday displacement
of the energy you have inside
so don't hide, just abide
these lines i'm about to send
it'll take time but we'll be in love again
and forget whether this is
the beginning or the end

she wrote: you are doing it again
playing my weaker side
you know how suave you are
and how easy i give in
but i love you too much
to let you have me
i deserve better and so do you
i deserve a man who promises me the world
and somehow seems to always come through
you deserve a girl like me
one who makes you feel
but you deserve a love based on something real
it's almost like you don't love me
just the idea of being in love
and it's something i hope you grow out of
but being your friend i can't
take advantage of your jaded eyes
to make you the man i want

he wrote: i'd hate to admit that i think you're right
but let's not give up

not this night
we have a chance to make this last
we have something amazing
and i have a simple question to ask:
will you let me be great for you?

she wrote: i need to go away
i need to take some time
i need to be with myself
but i'll leave you with this rhyme
it's from a song i know you know
'cause it meant something to me and you
and now it'll mean something more
so as i close the door
please let me go
this is something i have to do

"the day the rain falls
let it wash away past sins
the day the rain falls
when our new love begins
the day the rain falls
i'll never dream without some sleep
the day the rain falls
in my heart your love i'll keep
the day the rain falls
when we return from taking space
the day the rain falls
you'll look in my eyes
       & see your smiling face"

victory rose *
(or "if the black box recorder is orange
what else are they lying about?")

often
very often
when driving to work
    or any place
i'll be in my truck
    and stopped dead in traffic
the sun beating down
Sigur Rós' () playing
and i'll look around me
at the SUVs with the soccer moms
the construction workers
    with the nascar numbers
    in the back windows
    of their 1/2 ton trucks
the white guys in the rice burners
the black guys in the cadillacs
everyone on their cell phones
    or thumpin' their bass
i'll look around and feel
like i am the only one
who gets the punch-line
to the world's joke

... as the earth turns and moon rises *

somebody please tell me
what is the difference
between a 3-year-old kid
who lives two blocks away
whom i've never seen
and a 3-year-old kid in the middle east
whom i've never seen?

they're both children
neither know what life truly is
neither have become brainwashed by patriotism
neither have hatred burning in their hearts
        or minds

they just want love
they just want to play
they just want to be kids
so why do we cry when
the kid two blocks away skins their knee
        but don't shed a tear
when we the bomb the fuck out
of the middle-eastern kid?

buildup/breakdown
(or "home used to be wherever you were")

i'm in that place again
feeling the way i do sometimes
in that mood
where i sit and stare
and don't blink for hours
staring at the wall
feeling i could melt it with my eyes
instead it all bleeds white
and i see images displayed before me
the faces of the ones i've hurt
those words that people have said
i'm feeling that the world hates me
and that i don't have any friends
when this happens all i can think about
are the mistakes i've made

when this happens i just get in my truck
and drive away from the city
that filthy fucking place
with its sex-boards lining the highways
and jerk-off shops on every corner
it's so disgusting
i drive off into the country
into the middle of kansas
the dark fields
where there are no city (shitty) lights
the only glow is from the flaming orbs
        in the black sky
the burning of my heart
        and the fire in my eyes
i get so tense and pent up with rage
my face turns red
and it feels like i am drunk
it feels like i could piss fire
        and ejaculate lava
that if i tried hard enough
i could make my chest explode
and a younger version of me could pop out
a naked crying me
a young me before

before it all

before the corruption
before the lies
before the seduction
before the alcohol
before the useless sex
and the drugs
before the stench of life

i want to destroy everything when this happens
all of my possessions
i want to rip the skin from everyone's face
i'm tired of all of this
i'm so fucking tired of being like this
alone
so tired.

quo vadimus *
(or "we're friends, this is what we gear-up for")

through it all
        we fought
through it all
        we won
it doesn't matter where we've been anymore
it used to matter
but now all i care about is what
        we will see in the future
we came together
and saw so many things
the girls
the drugs
the empty bottles in our rooms
and all of that brought us nothing
        but an ending
you've called me every name in the book
and i've done the same to you
i went from willing to die for you
to wanting to kill you myself
we grew from being those two boys in the creek
to those tired men caught in the world's web
hands on each other's throats
we have grown away from each other
        and we came back
however we'll still eventually
come to the point where
        we'll talk once a year
if we're lucky
but we have a past
        a great one
and we struggled through the present
we have a future
and can make it as great
        as we choose to make it

through it all
through every failure
and every success
i still want to stand beside you

in the footsteps of alex troust
(or "you're nothing unless you're yourself")

i think you are all a bunch a fucking fakes
you are recreations of images
attempted clones of the famous
you try to be the posters on the wall
you try to become the guy on the stage
just because you wear a denim jacket
    and grow your hair long
    doesn't make you Kris Roe
just because you wear tight shirts
    and play piano
    doesn't make you Andrew McMahon
and you won't ever write anything close to "Konstantine"
just because you dye your hair black
    and wear black lace on your arms
    doesn't make you Davey Havok
and never try to be that guy from vendetta red
    he's a fucking douche-bag cunt!
you try to write about love
when you don't even know what it is
you've never felt it
and just because you've fucked 12 girls
doesn't mean you know shit about intimacy
just because you like songs about drugs and suicide
doesn't mean you are better at writing about them
    when you've never tried either
don't try to write the way
    the people you listen to do
you don't have it in you
you've never been there
not to imply you never will
listen to the words
    and hear the melodies
but don't try to mimic it
when you have no basis
    forget idolization
    forget looking up to emulate
just be yourself
write what you know
dress the way you dress
and someday

        some kid will want to be like you
before he too learns
      to be himself

jerking off in the reflecting pool

remember how a few years ago
there was this terrorist attack?
and people all bought it up
and became patriots for a day
and put those
"9/11 we will never forget" fifty-cent stickers
       on their $40,000 cars

why don't we see those stickers anymore?
oh, that's because the people took them off

i guess they forgot

the pebble minority
(or "the lonely atoms about to split")

we are in the chat rooms
the corners of coffee shops
under trees in the park
we look just like everyone else
except we think and feel
we don't live for today
our eyes are not fixated
on figures walking down red carpets
our eyes are on the page
the blank empire before us
soon to be filled
we scribble our thoughts and ideas
speak our minds through ink on paper

the majority parades in front of us
trying to disrupt our concentration
to make us conform and give in
become insiders

as the majority gathers in a stadium
and prays to their leader in the spotlight
we are the outsiders
up in the catwalks
hiding in the darkness
biding our time

we are so few
together we hardly weigh an ounce
our voices barely audible
but even the smallest rock
creates a ripple
that touches every shore
and breaks every wave

andala & the dildo of frozen tears

she fucks herself nightly
fingers wrapped around the shaft
gripping tight with knuckles white
she shoves it in
pulls it out
        (lather, rinse, repeat)
she's thinking of all the men
images of cocks in her head
remembering their lies
that got them in her bed
the promises
the vows
the propositions of a better life
taking every chance
on a chance
for a greater man
they all left her
used her and out the door
they all hurt her
this makes her feel sad
but at times she doesn't mind

when she sees them on the streets
after their "let's just be friends" phone call
after she swallowed their sperm
she likes to watch them squirm
they can't even look her in the eye
and this gives her so much power
it seems that she should be depressed
that she was used and forgotten
but she got a good lay (most of the time)
and so did they
but they were too cowardly
to reach for the better thing
they could have had the whole package
her heart, mind, and soul
but they settle for a drunken night
that will haunt them for the rest of their lives
she knows it is their loss
their fault for being pathetic

they have made her cry

and at times forced her to build a wall
but she can still get off to the memories
of their dicks
in her sweet little hole

she knows that she has become empowered
by their lack of balls to commit
but does she give a shit?
hell no
she fucks herself nightly
reminiscing about those assholes

the world of celluloid & flickering light

the last film just dropped
it's time to go home
leaving the memories of you here
the torment i feel & the
horrible thoughts of you out there
exploring the world without me
spending your nights in bed alone (hopefully)
the love we have is boxed up
resting high up on the closet shelf
existing only in that box
emotions floating around it
trying to hold onto those incredible emotions
like tying you to the bed & licking your every inch
indulging in your sweet flavor
gazing into your crystal eyes
holding your body close to mine
touching outside & in
steam coming off of us
climaxing in unison
and never wanting it to end
making love to you
everything fades away
only you & i
naked in the universe
uninhibited
never looking back
did you ever think it would end?
everything does
remember what we had
sweet dreams to you
take your time
and find yourself
never mind about me
don't worry about what i'll do
i'll be alone &
numb, eventually
getting back on my feet
to move on
however
understand that it's not truly over
really, we can have it back
someday

darling, you were (are) everything to me
and i want nothing else in the world, just
you

blue boy under a red moon

flickering lights on the walls of your room
on the very first night we ever touched
your lip gloss on my lips
and makeup on my shoulder
all of our time together
feeling so important
making love on your bed
blaring Something Corporate
smelling your perfume on the pillows
and your scent on the sheets
i want to dream about you forever
when you kiss me my knees go weak
when i'm not with you i can't think
        of what to do
i don't know where to go
when i'm all alone
and thinking of you

*this piece was thrown together using
unfinished pieces from
<u>understanding thursday</u>

troy's bucket*

good-bye to my family
so long my loved ones
my childhood has ended now
    all i had is gone
what happens on the road ahead
    you can never tell
i'm looking back
    and dreaming of
my 21 wishing well

the song said "tuesday's gone"
    and you never did believe
burning away our childish dreams
    and adolescent fears
destroy forgotten hopes
    to relive teenage years
put on 'Smokey & the Bandit'
    and toss me another beer
we don't know it yet
    but soon i won't be here

in the land of ivory bullets
    with sparkling chromium shells
i'm lost and being found
    still searching for
my 21 wishing well

    *this piece was an unfinished piece
    from <u>understanding thursday</u>

conception

forget the cold eyes
        that stare through you
and the whispers behind your back
it doesn't matter what they say
they'll never understand
everything they have was given to them
without ever having to lend a helping hand
they take what they have for granted
never having to work for shit
you are going to have to struggle
        and fight to make ends meet
this situation may not have been planned
        but it is far from a mistake
don't worry about where the daddy is
you can do this on your own
if people call you "worthless"
        or a "little whore"
say "fuck 'em"
        and prove 'em all wrong
become a great provider
        and a trusting friend
it doesn't matter if you're by yourself
it doesn't matter you're 16
it doesn't matter what you've done
        only what you're gonna do
i have faith in you
bringing a life into this world
is the greatest thing you could ever do
just earn the right to be called
a mother

suicide notes & straightened coat hangers
(or "the secrets we keep")

i know
you know
we both know all the dirt
the terrible things
we've messed up so much
the drunken drives
        and statutory fucks
the cheating
        and the drugs
you know where i've fallen
        'cuz you've been there too
i don't know what to think about anything
not anymore
we are not kids
we ventured all through this town
looking for excitement
looking for greatness
looking for something incredible
and along that trail
        we found all of that
but eventually we found
        where the sidewalk ends
and we stepped out of our shorts
        and school pride t's
into loafers
into suits
finances & responsibility
we know about the teenage partying
        and the shoplifting
the mindless vandalism
we know all of the lies
        and the cover-ups
if we turn on each other
with this knowledge we've attained
we will be the finest of enemies
but we don't
we just push on
and step into the future
trying to achieve something amazing
while looking at each other

        and smiling
seeing the understanding
        behind these tired eyes
knowing what we know
knowing what we know
we will have large families
nice houses
great lives
inside we'll know where we've been
we'll always know these things
and never speak of them

you know all of the shit i've done
        because i've told you
and you've heard it from others too
and just so you know
i'm aware
        of the one thing
        you've kept from me

whores don't deserve my heartbreak

kiss my eyelids
        with your razor-blade lips
grind your hips into my face
        so i can taste it all
i want to run my barbed-wire hands
        all over your skin
        and mark you as mine
red lines connecting all your appendages
fluorescent eyes
        stare us over
four-leaf clover pupils
poison tears dripping on my chest
        and your black-widow kiss
        gives me warmth
your cherry nipples in my mouth
your head heading south to fellate

stab your nails into my throat
as i squeeze my hands on yours
slam down on me
        and fuck me raw
run your icy hand through my hair
and dare me to bust inside you

your purpose of this night
        your only reason
is to try and control me
        use me
and make me hurt and fall
        seduce me with your ruse
you are trying to fuck me over
to feel better
        about all the jizz you swallowed
and the gallons shot on your face
tell me you love me
        to get me to say it back
i won't, bitch!
        but i'll play your game
what you don't know is
        the ball is in my court
my intentions are the same as yours
        my soul you'll never fucking take

maroon car my ass! *
(this mother-fucker is red!)

that glint off of your stainless steel skin
       gets me in the mood again
to pound that little twat of yours
smack it so it turns even pinker
       then red
you're so tough and strong
but you'll break when i take it out
you'll drop to your knees
       bowing to its girth
          enthralled by its glistening beauty
your taste buds excited
       mouth salivating
longing for its taste
       and its cream-filled surprise

_____**abhor-tion**
(or "a third-reich trimester termination")

this is the life we lead
        for a flag on a pole we bleed
with bikini-atoll tempers
exploding radiation
dark chernobyl hearts
murdering the young ones
raising these unfortunate sons
city youths in the jungle hold rifles
rich boys at home screwing whores
standing for an outdated anthem
a song that once stood for pride
now we hide behind our arms cache
lazy politicians
smoking cigars & sipping booze
losing the votes of their constituents
buy them back with false words
this is the life we lead
our lives are over long before we die
and we don't even try to make a difference
channel surf & flip the stations
images flickering in our eyes
subconscious voices telling us to buy
        subliminal lies
this is the life we lead
this is the life we lead
soon there'll be bodies hanging
        from the town square gallows
our heathen minds
        and savage thirst for blood
covered up by our red, white, & blue lapel pins
        and our silver cross chains
making new enemies with every fictitious war
upside-down frowns on our faces
when we see the live feed of the destruction
        from camel-fucker-ville
this is the life we lead
this is the life we lead

this is the life we are given
        and we follow the herd

        to the chopping blocks
we're all a bunch
        of stupid fucks

nine lives lived
(or "a black cataract derision")

do you see me?
do you see, do you see?
outside your house?
inside your mind?
do you feel me?
do you even feel?
i'm running circles in your brain
flicking my zippo to fire your synapses
your mouth closed tight
by the wires i'm pulling in your skull
you are the darkness
       and i'm the nucleus you surround
do you see me? do you see?
i'm looking out through your eyes
you look in the mirror
       and you don't smile
'cuz i won't let you
you draw in a breath
       like a child draws a tree
       straight and narrow
       with no feeling
do you even know i'm here?
outside your house?
inside your head?
feel this as i kick in your fucking brain!
taste this as i piss down your throat!
i'm your demon worm
and you can't get rid of me
'til you realize
you're a worthless piece of shit!!

woodstone & 81st

the boy swinging on the jungle gym
        is going to die today
i don't know if i should tell him or not
his mom is chopped up in my trunk
he has no one to go home to

ferlinghetti's seed

i am the boy on the merry-go-round
        always destined to do so
        and watch the calliope crash
i am the boy on the beach
        always running from the surf
i am the boy in the movie
        who will never get the girl
i am the boy in the painting
        who will never catch the lightning bug
i am the boy in the back of the room
        who'll never be remembered
i am the nameless
        & faceless me

emotional weapons of words
(or "beware o' sheep")

we are an isolation nation
a nation of boxcar lives
we surround ourselves with walls
    cramped lifestyles
i walk down the streets
    between the bodies
    the meat puppets
the overpriced stores like
    electric fences
    keep us locked in
celebrities & TV personalities
    man the guard towers
firing gossip at us from above

we are an isolation nation
a nation of boxed-in animals
i sit next to you in a diner
    and i smile
    you smile back
i smile when i really want to rip
    your fuckin' throat out
i want to break your nose
    with my fist
i don't care about your two-story
    or your subscription to 'us'
or your kid scoring the winning point
i don't care about you
you build up your walls
    of porn mags
    and julia roberts dvds
your suv and mini are your escape pods
i built my fort with novels
    and notebooks
    scarred with my horrid
    chicken scratch
my walls are stronger than yours
nothing can blow it down
you are a wolf and you huff
    and you fuckin' puff
but i don't fear you

you are a sheep in wolf's clothing
        you corporate rag doll
you can blow me
but can't destroy my world

rainbow socks with the individual toes
(or "that enthralling beauty i know")

i long to taste your chocolate eyes
        and smell your coconut skin
toss cares into the wind
        catch them
        and put them back again

find a dandelion and blow it
        through the air
watch them catch the breeze
        and mix with the uncaught cares

let me kiss your dewdrop lips
        moist from the cold morning
        moist from looking at me

grab my hand and squeeze it
        inhale the pollen
        exhale the joy
you are my lovely girl
        and i'm your love-struck boy

sisyphus' son
      (or "the pebble not quite a boulder")

magazine glory doll
      with the new-york wall-street clown
take a chance and think
stop and drink in your surroundings
see the talent boy
      with the hip-hop vibes
the uptown girl
      with the drugstore style
the aristocrat panhandler
      dealing in flesh
the trailer-park heartthrob
      with pecs to check your mate
midwestern prom queen
      with dreams to be a mother
and a brother in the army
      wanting to be back home
the drifter who roams
      from place to place
      seeing face to face
      eye to eye
and smoking the weed that's laced
seeing the colors never known
don't forget the weepy poet
      sitting at a table
      in the coffeehouse
with nothing to do but write
      about what he's not
who he has never met
      and what he'll never see
but he'll be writing
      when you're all dying
it's the only way
      he knows how to be

_____dio? who dis? dis ain't dr. dre?
tell the boy with scabby knees
        and bleeding elbows
to climb up on the roof
        and prove to the world
        that he exists
scream your lungs out
        to cause a blackout
for glory you must give it all

_____rorshach man
i am the ever-changing
        with the rearranging limbs
i change my way one day
        and put it back again
i mold to fit my surroundings
i adapt to what's around
i talk in the regional dialect
        that is accepting
adhere to the culture and sounds
i will rebuild myself
        'til you love me
tear apart and rip all down
i will be what you want me to be
if you'll be my friend
i have no one else in this town

living in the shadow of another
(or "facing the light and casting your own")

take all these things from me
    the images and phrases
    caught like a crook in my memory
destroy all the stuff i know
    the trivia and facts
    bits of info between the cracks
i wanna watch these things go
fed up with walking
    in these borrowed shoes
knowing what i do
    because i have nothing else
i wanna be myself
erase the celebrities names from my mind
    and the movie mistakes i find
i don't want to remember every detail
    every scent
    every feel
burn off my memorizational juices
    like excess oil in the fields
take all these things from me
what i was before today
replace my mind with the brain of a dip-shit
i wanna experience the bliss of ignorance
let me sleep an entire night through
    without poems, stories,
    & yet-to-be-filmed movies
    showing in my head
i don't wanna worry about my friends,
    stress over a job
erase it all so i can be stupid
    but free
i want to be a un-jealous lover
    and live my life as simple
    as a Cake album cover

ethereal tripsy
[or "my paranormal lost (last) love"]

their voices echoed through the house
    as if projected
        through gestapo loudspeakers
        their jabbering laughs
i was in bed
    tired from my nightly binge
    the darkness before
the door to my room closed
    soon to be opened
i was awaiting her arrival in my domicile
the stairs began creaking
    with the pain from their age
this house is almost the same age
    as me at 22
i felt her approaching
i've not seen her in months
i didn't know why she was here
doorknob jingled
    a little bit jangled
i closed my eyes
    pretended to be asleep
she came in
    dropped her purse to the floor
    like she used to do
    back when she was mine
pulling out the stool from beneath my desk
    she sat down
knowing my ruse she began to talk
wanting me to get up
    get out
go out and spend the day
    with her shopping and talking
    and "govereeting"
struggling not to smile or
    open my heavy eyelids
eyelids not kissed by her in years
we were going to a going-away party that night
    at her boyfriend's house
    my best friend's house
a party for another friend

he is going away
        leaving
like she once left me
i still kept up my game
        eyes closed
        breathing normally
she stopped speaking
i could feel her eyes on my body
a body she hasn't seen in years
her voice became different
        when she began again
more insecure
        more sedated
        monotone
the words she spoke
        she had practiced before
helping to delude herself
        and make it easier
        to get over us
"you know i am happier with him,
        he treats me the way
        i deserve to be treated" she said
"i love him and he loves me, unlike you.
        there was a time when i believed
        in what we had" she said
she knew i was awake
        and it became obvious
        because i began to breathe deeper
"open your eyes, please open them.
        i loved you, i did, but
        we never would've worked,
        we have to forget what we had."
i began to cry, sobbing hard
        breathing harshly
"please open your eyes, b"
(she always called me 'b' although
        i fucking hated it)
"please open your eyes"
i still kept them closed
        tears leaking through
i loved her
        i know i loved her
        and her me

but i ruined it
       i know this
       and i'm over it
i swear it
i don't love her like i did
       back in the days of gold
and she no longer cares for me
and i can accept that
"we have to forget what we shared,
       and try to be friends"
i kept sobbing and crying
i loved what we were so much
"please open your eyes, brett"
and i knew i couldn't
i loved her but was so afraid
i knew what i'd find if i opened them
i cried and she sat there
       begging me to look at her
i was so afraid
       but i opened them to find
       she was no longer there
       she never was
       she was a dream
she is the memory of
       "a girl i once knew"
a girl whose ghost
       i'll always live with in my head
and that is my penance
       for what i did to her

between clifton & coleridge
(or "where the gravel meets the dirt")

faces of the women i knew
    and their names
float around
    in circles
    like cig. ash
    in the cab of my truck
driving the writhing black streets
the tunnels of darkness
    lined by trees
    & street walkers
alone in this world
alone in my mind
windows down
    the absolute-zero chill
    seeping through
not affecting me
there is a bit of blood
    in my alcohol stream
keeping me warm
keeping me alive
brown stains on the roadside
hiding children in the bushes
    throwing rocks
i used to be one of those kids
dodging the high beams
    cruising in circles
    breathing in spurts
still making progress
still gaining yardage
still exhaling carbon dioxide
keeping the trees alive
where is it i went?
where did i go?
i can't remember
    any of the last half hour
the music was so loud
    i couldn't hear the sirens
i don't know why
    my windshield is cracked
    like a psyche patient

i don't know why
    i taste blood
    between my teeth
my chest feels bruised
    & i can't move my toes
i inhale the stench of alcohol
    while blood seeps out my nose
where did i go?
what happened?
who is that on my hood?
i need to stop and think
    perhaps down another drink
wipe the shattered glass from my eyes
    with fallen leaves
where i've been
    & what happened
you'll never believe

five crappy band haiku

(the haiku are crappy, not the bands)

rock Rx Bandits
lyrical hardcore gang-bang
burn the venue down

Celebrity's here
gonna show you how it's done
hear it, change your world

Something Corporate
the great ballad "Konstantine"
it's all good to me

Early November
wherever you play i'll be
belt out "Sunday Drive"

icelandic epics
amazing stars Sigur Rós
you are music gods

cunts without a clue

the other day
i saw this sticker
in the back window of
some mother-fucker's truck
it said:
"want another 9-11? vote democrat!"

what the fuck is wrong with people?
9-11 happened
and yes, it shouldn't have
but what the fuck?
it's no one's fault

those people didn't die
because of the previous political party
or any party

political parties are bullshit!
why have two groups
fighting each other
when we could have one
fighting for a better country?
a greater world?

how could someone
exploit the cold-blooded murder
of 3000+?
(plus the thousand more murdered
in the aftermath in afghanistan)
i'm not smart
i don't know much
i couldn't do anything
to make this world better
but i do know
that when i look around
and see people pointing fingers
and blaming each other
for the spilt blood of the innocent
i want to cry

for this is the world
i am to bring my kids into?

thursday wakes up silent ...
i want to believe Geoff
when he sings "we are cured, we are cured!"
he's a good man
        and normally i'd accept his word
but the air in my lungs, it burns
the taste in my mouth is sour
for the people who want
        to kill us all
are the people
        with all the power
the tears falling from my cheek
        are weak liquid particles
atoms escaping from my face
giving chase to a forgotten idea
i don't wanna c ya
after the final solution is performed
        and the deformed minds
        take control of your will
passing pernicious bills
        on capitol hill
while we gargle seminal swill
        shot across our teeth
like lies injected
        with batches of belief
none of this makes sense
        should i lament?
        or repent?
walk in these shoes
        of sovereign cement?
to sink in a river of deceit
        and not think before i eat
swallowing this 5 (inter)course
        naked lunch
i have a hunch
that i'll soon be
        in the belly of the beast
or at least
        crawling up its throat
tossing out a note
        a letter of acceptance
        sealing my fate
as of late

i don't really feel
        like fighting the power anymore
just giving in and bending over
        sucking it
        like a whore

curtain / lights up
(or "the beginning of act ii")

i now know who i am
and what i'm supposed to be
i've changed, transformed, reborn anew
do you have what it takes
        to stand here next to me?

i will never again feel bad for
        all those fucked-up things i did
i paid my debt
and did all i could
to make it up to all of you

i don't fucking care if you like my first book
        my second or my third
i won't defend or protect my art
        or stand up for what i wrote
but i also won't apologize for a single line
i'm going to keep writing
        keep reading
        keep on this track
        of rebuilding myself
you do what you gotta do
i still care in a way
you're all still my friends & enemies
but i'm not going to rearrange
everything for you
not anymore
i'm not going to let you keep me here
in your day-to-day routines
one by one i'm crossing off items
on my list of hopes & dreams

looking back at who i was
simply three short years ago
i can't even recognize myself
and if you can't accept
what i've become
then you can go fuck yourself
i am the combined efforts of everything
        i have read & seen

and everyone i've ever met
you're responsible for the creation of me
       but from now on
i'm gonna be what i wanna be
love me or deceive me

i plan to write a dozen books
       and shoot a film or two
all to make you proud of me (kind of)
while i'm still waiting
       to be proud of you

soixante-neuf

my tongue is writhing
running up & down your slit
your scent is enthralling
with my nose rubbing on your clit
your taste is like a thousand cherries
oh, it's so sublime!
and when you climax it becomes tangy
like suckling a tiny lime

dig your nails into my kneecaps
the pleasure/pain is magnifique
i'll return the masochistic favor
with a little spank to both your cheeks
inhale deep & open wide
take as much of me as you can in
give this a few more minutes, maybe five
and i promise to make you cum again

people call this perverted
        lusting of the flesh
        a sin
but with you i can't think
        of any better
        position to be in

without the darkness there is no light
(even if the light doesn't shine)

the squealing of the faucets
and rushing of the water awoke him
sitting up in bed
looking through blurry eyes
his wife was washing her hands
the cold water on her fingers
and soap suds in the sink
he now could hear the toilet
refilling with water

"what time is it?" he asks
"about 2:30," she answered
"why are you up?"
"i had to pee."
he lays back down
stuffing the pillow tight under his head
she says "i'm gonna go downstairs
and get a small snack."
he grunts an okay
she walks out of the room
he slowly
slowly fades
back into the realm of sleep

minutes later he hears a crash
a scream
his heart jumps to his throat
his body jumps out of bed
"debra?! ... debra?!? honey?"

silence ...
silence ...

his heart pounds
his blood races
his hands and body shake
kneeling down he braces himself
with one hand against the bed
the other hand reaching underneath
"sweetie, is everything okay?!"

something shatters
as his hand grabs the gun
slowly creeping towards the door
he hears a commotion downstairs
another scream

he swallows his heart
puts it back where it belongs
and rushes down the stairs
he gets to the kitchen
flips on the light
to see ...

debra is lying on the floor
chocolate ice cream and an empty bowl
      lying next to her
blood oozing from her throat
she doesn't move
he stands there looking down at her
he's almost convulsing

suddenly a hand grabs him from behind
he is stabbed in the side
he throws his weight back
and flings the attacker aside
and turns around and fires two shots
both hit the attacker
in the chest

he stands there
looking down at this man
trying to breathe
then looks at his wife
who no longer can
his eyes are still blurry
"is this a dream ... ? a nightmare?"
he steps forward
and fires one last round into the attacker's face

he drops the gun to the floor
and walks in a daze
back upstairs
clutching his bleeding side

back to his bedroom
over to the sink
he looks down to see
the soap suds still there

paseo

downtown streets
    of a pothole nation
oil-marked & gravel-ridden
    with sneakers on the tele-wires
sitting on the crumbling curve
    a young negro boy
picking at his bare, calloused feet
looks up at me
    my white skin
he says, "i don't see a difference"

_____ minute deliberation before extreme & blatant pontification

tempers rise
igniting like flames
      to spark in the eyes
      & ejaculate tears
devoting prominence
declaring a promenade!
oh, hark! to the max!
desire & flatulence!
ticky-ticky with the time
to rhyme, wine & dine
explode the drums
      & pluck the strings
piano wire lashes
      falling from your face
fire burning
      a glowing hearth
"Also Spake Zarathustra"
projecting from the phonograph
arms outstretched
      fingers curled
      back arched
shadow cast like
      a fisherman's bait
catching onto the joke
      whose punch-line
      dangles in the air
like the 82 man from the gallows
      on all hallow's eve
deceiving the masters
shriek a shrill "oh, please!"
touch me 'til no one sees
trumpets blare
and we're here
naked in the sea
oh, glory!
rapture!
atrocity!
to decree!
it's time to start
      my final solution
bow on your knees
      to me

to live & die in a.a.

lonely hirsute woman
sitting at her desk
fragile fingers poking keys
ink printed on paper
red eyes & nicotine-stained teeth
smell of smoke in all her hair
stench of liquid & roses
        a bouquet of vodka & sweets
typing
click clack!
        clackety click!
bandage on her forearm
soaked all the way through with blood
sniffing mucous back up her nose
downing a pill or two
        percoset & vicodin
gulps down coffee with a shot
        of the bouquet vodka
type type-ity!
        type-ity type!
lamenting, frustrating
prophesying
        things to come
 a few more pecking stabs
        at the keys
        and she'll be done
the words & voice
        of a former lover
run looped
        & loopy in her skull
"say good-bye, 'cuz i'm leavin',
        i can't stand you anymore."
that woman used to love her
and she still loves her back
typing out an apology
        an "i'm sorry"
an "i'll never have you back"
with a type type-ity!
        clickity clack!
pausing, breathing, exhaling
looking out the window
a pigeon shitting on her railing

"time to take a dive," she says
        clack clickity!
pulls the paper from the carriage
        rolls it tight & sighs
downs the last of the vodka
        shoves the letter down
        the bottle's neck
opens the window
        tosses the bottle
        into the breeze
dives off of the railing
        and races it to the ground
the pigeon (done shitting)
flies into the apartment
        & lands on the typewriter
pecks & pecks & pecks at the keys
"... the end."

tryst
(or "tryst")

a short one
not many words
listen
tell me where it hurts
i can't apologize enough
for killing you
but i want to live
so you can't
i'm weak and feel threatened by you
so i stabbed you in the back
too bad
so sorry
good-bye

hi without the coup
next time you're riding
or driving in a car
put it on cruise control
crawl out the window
onto the roof
ride it like a skateboard
and leap into the air
dive
try to fly
see if the angels catch you
and take you with them

_____ **caesura**

sitting on my front porch
        birds chirping
sun fading
        breeze blowing

i used to write a lot
        sitting here
        years back

back as a high-schooler
back as new blood
        to the real world

i wrote "time" here
        and all of those pieces
        for my friends
Will, Kirk, Tim, & Caroline
back in the days of 'til the streetlights came on
        four years ago
four lives ago
back when Marilyn was mine
back when my parents were still together
back when my brother was a marine
things have changed so much
        in four years
except the front porch
it is still very inviting
        calming, welcoming

back when i used to write here
        i was always
        thinking about the present
        never the past
i never thought i'd still be
        writing on this porch in 2004
it never crossed my mind
but now at 22 and not dumb 18
i think about 2000
        and how i won't be writing here
        in 2008

i wrote "the tether ball ding" here

        back in 2002
and that was the last one i wrote here

two years?

it hasn't even been a year since i finished
        understanding thursday
but the life detailed in that book
        seems so far away

hell, in three months it'll be
        the one-year anniversary
        of the publishing of
        'til the streetlights came on

although that version of the book sucks

where will i be in 2005?
where will i be in 2008?
fuck i have no idea
but without a doubt
        there will always be
        somewhere inviting
        for me to sit
        & write
        & reminisce
about what i am losing every day

in 2001 or 2002 that would've frightened me
but after "understanding" i really do
        understand

and now in april of 2004
        the days of
        ars gratia artis
i am no longer afraid of
        what lies ahead
& when i cross those paths
        & take those turns
you will be coming with me

assholes & accolades

i am not great
never have been great
never done anything great
never will i be great
nor will i ever do anything great

all i have is a pen
    & a black book
        with my heart in words
i write for me
    it's all i have
that is wholly mine

if i had an audience
    which i don't
i'd hope it wouldn't be
    those bourgeois fucks
who read & only read
the top 5 books
    at the moment
they read the clear
    clean-cut poetry
    from collins
    or angelou
or any other "poet laureate"
having awards & praise
    doesn't make me
    enjoy your work
    anymore than normal

i don't want people to read my shit
because some 'Annie Hall'-esque
    new york brainiac
    socialites
thinks it is so urban
    & risqué
so startling
    & unique

fuck that
    & fuck them!

if i had a choice
i'd only allow my work
      to be read by
the kids
      people
sitting in their dark rooms
computer screen glowing on them
underground music playing

someones who would understand my work
      for what is says
      not what it is
if that makes sense

if those kids have a choice
between a joint
      bottle of pills
      a razor & their skin
or a few of my shitty poems
and they choose my shit
instead of cutting themselves up

then my job is done

i don't need any awards or accolades
to make me proud of my creations

truth

i have to admit
that i love your sadness
and i'm glad
i'm not the cause of it

waiting on a brand new midnight

i don't know why
i don't know why i am crying
i don't know why
i don't know why i am dying
        to be there with you
i don't know why
i don't know why i am losing
        the brightest star in my night sky
and i don't know what to do
        alone & crying here without you

i'm waiting on a brand new midnight
        watching the rain fall down
i'm waiting on a brand new midnight
        she's running all over this town
i'm waiting on a brand new midnight
        she's one in a million you see
i'm waiting on a brand new midnight
        'cuz she means everything to me

all those cold nights
        naked in your bed
lyrics from "Globes & Maps"
        playing in our heads
and what i remember
        is how you once said
"because of moments like this"
and then we kissed with the stars above
looking down at us
        basking in our love

all the time at home all alone
i don't know what to do
even armor for sleep
        won't protect me
            from dreaming of you
we had no reason to end
so i'm waiting to begin again
i'll let you go
if you tell me where you'll be
and as long as you know
you can always "say anything" to me

my sweet punk-rock girl
with that Ingrid Bergman smile

i'm waiting on a brand new midnight
        watching the rain fall down
i'm waiting on a brand new midnight
        she's running all over this town
i'm waiting on a brand new midnight
        she's one in a million you see
i'm waiting on a brand new midnight
        'cuz she means everything to me

it sometimes seems that
i have no life without you
and there's no other way to be
because you're life to me
come back someday to hold me tight
as "we rise on sun beams & fall in the night"

and no matter what
through all of the fights & the lies
you shall always remain
the brightest star in my sky

because you're life to me
because you're life to me
because you're life to me
because you're life to me

i'm waiting on a brand new midnight
it will be a sight to see
when she comes back, loving
kissing & making me
the happiest man you've ever seen

i've held on to this hope for so long
        but still we're fading like this song

your feature presentation will begin momentarily
(or "pulling the plug from the dam")

waiting
always waiting
we're always waiting
for what?
why do we sit here?
thumbs either twiddling
        or up our asses

biding
always biding
we're always biding our time
we all harbor the power
        to do & say & create
        anything we want
but we don't
we're scared
why?

we all are amazing
        but we hide

in chat rooms
        and through text messages
we spill our guts
bare our souls
but no one really sees

we need
need
we fucking need
        & must
must shut off the computer
smash those fucking phones
        against the wall
and grab our books of written word
        & make them spoken

stand on our roofs and yell
        "i am here!"
        "this is what i have to say!"

i look back at history
at everyone who made a difference
    or started a generation
Kerouac & Ginsberg
    & all those beat cats
they were around my age
    when they changed society
they completely shattered
    all of the rules of writing
but what was it about them?
why were they the ones to do it?
because they were so smart?
they were smarter than me
    that's true
was it because they were talented?
    perhaps, once again, they were
more talented than i'll ever be
but there were and are
    millions of people
    smarter & more talented
    than them
so how did they do what they did?
what was it?

it was guts & balls
they were fearless
    completely unafraid
they just did what they did
    & said what they had to say
not caring about perception
    or about what is correct or not
they weren't afraid of their weaknesses
completely unashamed of what they were
either alcoholics, druggies,
    or queers
they had the strength to say
    what they felt they should
that is why they are remembered
    & that is/was why they were great

are you great?
can you be?

or are you still afraid?
can you log off
    & go to a poetry reading?
or submit your work to a publisher?
or let a peer take a look?

i wanna be great
    & i'm ever so slowly
    gaining that courage
to step into the world
    with my thoughts & words blazing
i wanna change this place
    & if i fail okay
but i'll fail trying
rather than be
    a failure while hiding

words & passwords

sparkling crescent smile
moonlit eyes cry
ready to sigh & scream
baby doll singing
wringing her dripping clothes
young child writing
bleeding some poetry & prose
this is, to me, how it seems
this is the killing of our dreams

tranquil nights of colloquial lies

i am covetous
i am a lover of beauty
i am a jealous man
i am all that you need
all i want is a lady
& kiss her the way
        she deserves
dazzle her with my fingers
        & comfort her
           with my words

i miss you so much Kelly

april 16th, 2004 - friday

i just want to be the final piece
    in the puzzle
        that is your jigsaw heart

something rarely said

i just wanna say:

i am proud to live in the suburbs
i am proud to be middle class
i am proud to be male
i am proud to be white

passive crossover
    (or "equalization of the solar-cells")

rupture this heart
the sun is casting
    looks & wicked glares
i sweat & dream
for nothing is
    what it seems
lightning rays
    & moon beams
echoes flicker
    sound waves fade

in the days of the invincible youth

weekend drunken benders
alcoholic teen dreams
rage-filled machines
stereos blasting
drugs lasting
as the clothes come off

with a lick & a touch
        a two-handed toss off
double teaming finger cuffs
puffing on the cock
        like a stogie

being fourteen with your parents gone
        rocks!

live for today
contracting diseases
        die tomorrow
what else is there to say?

just have fun
there are no consequences
        for your actions

puke drying on shag carpet
girl lying when parents return
cigarette burns in the sofa
used condoms under the beds

what goes through our heads?

_____**freedom fries**
(or "the all-american all-stars")

he doesn't know he is going
       to become a junky
       in two years
       & overdose in three
she doesn't know she is going
       to fall in love tomorrow
       & be heart broken
       in six months
he doesn't know his mom
       will kill herself
       in two weeks
she doesn't know her son
       wants her to die
he doesn't know his girlfriend
       is sucking another cock
       right now
she doesn't know the cock
       she is sucking
       has syphilis
he doesn't know he has syphilis
       & will spread it
       to three more mouths
       & cunts
she doesn't know she is gonna
       lose her virginity
       tomorrow night
       & that it won't
       be by choice
he doesn't know he is gonna
       lose control
       & rape his girlfriend
she doesn't know she's gonna
       marry a future pedophile
he doesn't know he will eventually
       molest his daughter
she doesn't know she will
       slowly poison her husband
       over the course
       of four years
he doesn't know he is gonna

                drive drunk
                & kill a family
                of five
she doesn't know what love is
he doesn't know how to love
she doesn't know she is gonna
                be buried in a barrel
he doesn't know he is gonna
                discover his sister's body
                buried on their farm
she doesn't know her first drink
                will lead her to
                a hundred random rooms
                & to dozens
                of anonymous meetings
he doesn't know his first joint
                will burn down his house
she doesn't know that
                sperm donor #3z95
                is her brother
he doesn't know that
                tomorrow he
                isn't going to wake up
she doesn't know her father
he doesn't know his mother
she doesn't do anal
he doesn't know he
                is gonna make her
she doesn't know that
                the tele-marketer
                that called her
                was her long-lost father
he doesn't know the gun he bought
                when he was 22
                will blow out the brains
                of his son, when
                he is 7
she doesn't know the man
                she has been sleeping next to
                & calls her "husband"
he doesn't know his daughter is being
                double-teamed right now
she doesn't know her son

        is jerking off
        to gay porn

he doesn't know why
        when he closes his eyes
        to write
        this is what he sees
he doesn't know why
        it doesn't bother him
        anymore

he doesn't know

brett-fly & the kelly-goat
(or "i'll never stop loving you")

when i dreamed of us
    i saw many more kisses
    before going to sleep
    & a lot more waking up
    in the middle of the night,
    & making love,
    without saying a word
when i dreamed of us
    i saw your starry eyes
    filled with tears,
    as i was down on bended knee
    with a ring held out before you
(not that it was ever planned, but i knew how
    i was going to propose & it would've
    been incredible)
when i dreamed of us i saw a lifetime
    of "i love you" & "i love you, too"
    a lifetime of me saying "you're beautiful"
    & you telling me to "shut up"
when i dreamed of us i imagined
    coming home from work
    to find a blanket laid out on the living room floor,
    music playing, a glowing fire,
    & your naked body,
    waiting for me
when i dreamed of us i saw
    our small wedding,
    with our drunk friends yelling,
    & our moms crying
    & i saw our honeymoon with
    three nights of hot sex
    under a cool moonlit sky
when i dreamed of us i saw
    a thousand nights of you & i
    lying in bed watching old TV shows
    on dvd,
'Friends', 'The West Wing',
    & 'Family Guy',
    me liking them
    & you telling me i'm stupid

when i dreamed of us i saw you
    saying over & over that we were never gonna
    have any kids,
    but you'd give in
    & when you held the first one
    in your arms
    & looked at me
    i'd be seeing you at the happiest
    point in your life,
    i'd see my child's new mother
    (you'd make a terrific one)
when i dreamed of us i saw
    a garage with my
    little economy car to get me to work,
    your suv for taking the kids
    to piano and baseball,
    & your hot little sports car,
    i'd hear you saying over & over
    how they're yours
    & i can't touch them
    & how sexy i would find you
    & your hardheadedness
when i dreamed of us i saw you & me
    building our children's beds
    & book shelves,
    you holding our baby
    as i read to him/her
    & our other children,
    the animal mobile spinning
    & casting shadows on the walls,
    walls painted like the sky & clouds
    (which you chose)
when i dreamed of us i saw images
    of long talks in bed,
    after tucking the kids in, followed
    by an hour of me
    watching you as you sleep,
    facing each other, me inhaling
    the breath your exhale,
    and not wanting it any other way
when i dreamed of us i saw myself
    walking into our bedroom
    on a day you stayed home sick from work

                (knowing you though, this would be rare)
                i'd see the blanket
                draped over the window,
                the room filled with a blue hue,
                i'd see you there & flashback
                to the day i visited you
                after the car wreck,
                i'd think about how far we've come
                & how we did this
                together
i'd watch you sleeping, your hair not washed,
        your nose red from the rough tissues
(which you bought even though
        i wanted to splurge and get
        the softer ones)
        you'd sneeze & cough up phlegm
        & i'd still see
        my beautiful wife
when i dreamed of us i saw you
        caring for our kids,
        skinned knees & broken hearts,
        we'd watch them fall
        & get back up again,
        there'd be recitals, concerts
        & tournaments,
        yelling, screaming,
        & telling us they hate us,
        fender benders, broken windows,
        & an arrest or two,
        but we'd raise them right
        & they'd be okay and go on
        to do such amazing things
because you're amazing,
        and maybe i'll be too
when i dreamed of us i saw a house
        outside the city,
        where i could write,
        & you could have a horse
we'd become too old for most things
        & the kids will come by
        & do yard work for us
        & we'd fix them lemonade,
        then spoil their kids

when i dreamed of us i saw us old
    but happy, always talking about what
    we did together,
    back in the days of our youth,
    getting caught in that skate park
    parking lot, making out,
    then talking about how much
    we have changed
    for the better
when i dreamed of us i was so happy
when i dreamed of us it gave me the strength
    to face each rainy day
    & although we're not together anymore
    and we may never have these things,
    & i'll feel the pain of missing them all,
i still thank you for sharing a part
    of your life with me
    & giving me something
    so powerful
    so incredible

something that made me dream

born only knowing to love

parked on the roadside
        highway stretching by
black sky above
my tongue on yours
        fingers inside you
your tongue on mine
        fingers wrapped around me
headlights bathing our naked
        bodies with radiance
filled with pleasure

is this the meaning of life?

the return of the master

low-brimmed black hat man
  trench coat flapping in the wind
diamond-tipped cane
  rapping on the ground
i look at him
  & then look again
not believing my eyes
chest sinks as heart goes weak

"i killed you," i said
"ay, but a wound, sir" he says
  "and i've been in an
  incapacitated state"
he raises his head & grins
streetlights showing me
  his skull-e face
his black teeth grind on each other
he spits
  "and me convalescence is at an end, sir"
  he says
"i'm not what i was back in those days
  when you were my leader,
  i have surpassed you"
"ay, you have," he laughs "but you'll never
  truly be free of me"
he laughs again, a deep hoarse,
  guttural laugh
coughing up smoke from his obsidian lungs
"you needed my help," he says
  "to fight those demons of yers"
"i fought them and they have gone"
"yes, but i still here," he says "you still need me"
"no, i don't. i am stronger than anything
  you have ever seen"
"we'll see my son, we'll see"
  and his body scatters like ash
  & i turn and walk away

   ... to be continued ...

school yard salvo

jungle gym shrapnel
        impaling 8-year-olds
bloody limbs on the merry-go-round
hand gripping monkey bars
        with no body attached
decapitated heads
        rolling down the slide
bullet-ridden bodies
        falling from the swings
loose eyeballs filling sandboxes
ripped off toes in the
        hopscotch square
blood pooling in the corner
        of the four-square box
childhoods blown apart

3:19

he grabs her lipstick
        & makes an X over his heart
so her malicious words
        (cyanide-tipped bullet encapsulations)
will be sure to hit their target

the cause for a cure

disaster & aggravation
        douche-bag façade
covering a scared child inside

suicides & contemplation
intimidation at the door
        of mystified assassinations

weeping long-haired mothers
sleeping in piles
        like bodies at auschwitz
mourning children
        with sky-blue pupils
        & blood-red smiles
yellow tears
        on green-hued skin

sweet dreams for the copacetic clique

slowly closing in
surrounding to attack
wicked beasts
    with rabid grins
slobbering foam
    from their snarling mouths
they are animals
they are animals
    in the wrappings of humans
clothes covering fur
leather gloves encasing
    razor-sharp talons

i stand on a precipice
    about to fall
dirt clumps breaking away
descending from the blue
    to the brown
these animals
    look like humans
but they thirst for blood
they don't understand
    what i am
they don't condone
    my lifestyle

their cult
their faction
their cell
their sect
    coven
    covey
    group
    society
    murder
don't care about my life

my race scares them
i make them question themselves
they do not feel secure
    with my open-minded
    & accepting kind

walking the same streets
       as their babes
       kids
       cubs
       children

they are going to slaughter me
cut my head from my heart
because they fear me

all so they can sleep tonight
my blood on their hands
       & their bibles
        under the pillows

lanky & pretentious
(or "i know i am but what are you")

i am in a room
        other flesh-piles around
that are supposedly called "people"

the girl with the bleach-blonde hair
        & tanned-leather skin
two pounds of make-up
        & gallon of perfume
mouth a-flappin'

the guy with the frosted tips
        cleft chin
        silver watch, sea shell necklace
        & khaki shorts
white teeth a flashin'

the tattooed goth chica
        pierced nips
        red streaks in
        her jet-black hair
thinking about cuttin'
        & wishing she was the pretty blonde
ranting about The Rapture

the computer nerd
        with the Vivaldi t-shirt
denim shorts that used to be jeans
pimply face spittin' out disses
        on the cleft chin guy
        (hoping he doesn't hear)

everyone is spouting gibberish
conversing about themselves
mindless conjecture

the scruffy-faced poet
        with crooked yellow teeth
pimply back
        & dry scalp
sits in the corner

judging them all
thinking he is better
but knowing he's not
he is just a separate piece
        cut from the same pie
everyone is spoutin' gibberish
everyone is talkin' aloud

so who the fuck is listenin'?

just the judgin' prick of a poet
        & he really doesn't give
                a shit about changing the world

masticating his testibles

reading light casting shadows
silhouette bombarding walls
his contour painting the room
    in black over forest green
the fan overhead blows
a voice sighs from the speakers
    a song
      something about
      "love will find a way"

cut-outs & pictures from magazines
    pinned to the shadowed walls
boxers down at his ankles
    knees burning on the rug
body hunched over
    in a prayer position

cool breeze blowing his hair
caressing his throbbing manhood
arm vibrating back & forth
    like a piston
imagining the girls that came before
    & dreaming of the girls
    who will come after
eyes closed
    breathing deep
    heart pounding
2:35 a.m.
    the rest of the household asleep
he sighs
    & then
    release!!

the visions fade
    breathing slows
    heart resumes
    its normal rhythm
looking down at the toilet tissue
    in front of him
    on the floor

he is just a boy

             in a dark
             shadow-filled room
in the suburbs
in the middle of the country
in this world
alone & tossing off

cathedral

when i see you
       i know you're truly happy
but often i can see
       something   someone
banging on the back
       of your stained-glass-window eyes
begging to be let out
begging to be heard
but you keep them trapped
       and don't let them
       utter a single word

understanding thursday

tears watering the land
        and constantly fading time
so i give in to the darkness
        i want to burn my memories
fuck a cheerleader
        a bottle of rum and
        some reefer to make the day begin
fuel my rage with your lyrical sex
        eat me and enjoy
i just want to know you
        on the battlefield of creation
years may pass before i earn either
        a cold december night
heartless angels strap on their gravity boots
        dreaming the pain of tomorrow
a frozen boy with a voiceless scream
        nor will i ever be
your love and trust
        screaming in her mind
depleting hope
        take a chance with redemption
genocide of the outsiders by the masses
        days go by and things can only change
of their conflict and pain
        your religion sealed airtight?
the treasures of a childhood reborn
        fuck fight your friends
commit me. please?
        i built my wall
all is fun in numbers
        a small tingle where you touched me
now it's time to talk about "some day"
        feeling the mounting depression
at my cowardice and begging
        whore-buying and junk-addictions
killing the places i fucking love
        so tall they scrape the heavens
i know i do it too
        touch your lips to mine
to see one night through in you
        don't say the words "we're done"
live for every second

        it all ends with a bang
your end will be coming
        friends are your downfall
it's hard not to hurt you
        because i'm struggling not to love you
        too soon i fell from grace
this moment forever yesterday
        nobody really liked him
(touch the light)
        a universe away
which we will never share
        what i looked like naked?
your kisses on my eyelids are forever
        i've done more than you
we burned for two years
        the pumping of their crotch
i will laugh at their pain
        what has life done to you?
and destroy our past
        my frankness and brutality
the one above only loves
        in the gun went and out his brain came
how can i make it through the night?
        ... a frozen shell of a once warm man
why can't you save me?
        "because of moments like this"
and she can't remember his name
        i held you and kept you warm
and losing you
        it brought my past back to me
i love knowing that we earned this
        only together for eternity
his feet dangle from above
        why wait 'til i'm 3,000 miles away?
teen blood fills flasks
        in the past i see us golden
no tears or cries for the martyr
        you end our midnight trysts
and together we were made impure
        in his face i stick my rage
in his paradise all will be behind you
        forget their dreams and dance
all i've done is think about you

everything in my life is a story
and you don't seem to care
to that guy's house
and she was
crescent moons on gravy trains
and bomb tenements in far off lands
and left me with a sticky face
as i've left and you love another
and now a new generation does
of deceptions and lies
i'm a 46-year-old virgin in rehab
i think executions should be an olympic sport
graced by your stars above
is it mere discretion or sheer indifference
why we fuck and why we share
and all things said
wishing to always be young
i don't doubt a dazzling bride you'd make
it is atmospheric and mystical
there is nothing in-between
i just never stopped loving back then
to check up on the cunts
with trust-fund babies and date rapists
you are my celluloid dream
the angelic hum of a streetlight
reminds me of you
because the stars will look at you
until we fix what we caused
... and for now that is all i need to understand.

part three

losing a love.
ending a friendship.
coming full circle.
looking ahead.
not wanting to make the same mistakes.
holding my head up high.

fighting a lonely war
(a farewell to Kelly)

and it begins
the cease-fire has broken
        peace is gone
           welcome chaos

hanging up the phone
        & collapsing to the floor
so we're truly done
you are with someone new
doing things with him
        that you've only done with me

i haven't felt like this in three years
i cracked open
        heart shattered
          & lying on the ground
tears escaping
my cries, echoing all around

i loved you so much
now all i have
        is visions of your body
with someone else inside you
        and i want to vomit

i vowed years ago to never again
        feel this way
never let anything, anyone
        affect me like the last girl
but i loved you so much more
        & this pain hurts 10x worse

you fucking broke me!
you fucking broke me!
i've cried very little the past few years
holding back a dozen tears
but haven't broke until now
        & i fucking broke because of you

you fucking broke me

my tears soaking my hands
        like "raindrops"
        in that song you love

it's easy for me to fall in love
but so hard to fall out
girls always complain about men
        not being able to commit
that's because it's easy for girls
        to walk away from love
while the men are left feeling like shit

i want you to look up
look up at the night sky
while i sit here & wait
do you see all those stars?
the ones i once compared you to?
watch as i destroy them all
        & pull the remainder from your eyes
i am going to implode them
so you can never have them
create black holes
        like the one in my chest

i'll be here waiting
        while you're out there
        with him

i won't allow myself to think about you
and i've already erased your number
        from my phone

what is so great about love?
you always lose it
        & it makes you
            never wanna love again

i am so stupid
i am such a fucking fool
all i ever did was be great to you
        & treat you
            the way you deserved
gave you everything you wanted

        & loved you as much as i could
so i guess it was obvious to see
        that i don't deserve you

it's funny isn't it?
        my imbecilic notions
while i'm hear writing poems for you
        about what i dreamed for us
        & how amazing i thought you were
you were in bed with someone else
that just goes to show me
that this is what you get
        when you try your hand
        at love

i now kind of wish i had hurt you
        or used your body
        to merely get off
i wish i would've hit you
        or not appreciated you
that way the pain i feel would be
        somewhat justified

what i feel right now
        makes me
        hate & regret
everything we ever did
        & had

i'm happy i don't have
        that many pictures of you
that way there is less
        for me to burn
not like i really would though

you once asked me
        how many girls had i
        had sex with on the bed
        we shared
i was surprised but proud
        to answer "two"
you and the other "girl i once knew"
        & i thought how interesting

that the only girls to share that bed
    were girls i truly loved

ironically yesterday i bought a new bed
    & today i learn you slept
    with someone new
so now the slate has been wiped clean
    & the next girl i'll fuck
    on my bed
    will surely
    never be
    you

in this you won
    & i lie defeated
heading off to fight
    in the next stage of this war

i guess i shouldn't rely on you
    to save me anymore

black dog blues

another time of my life is over
      so i write it down
      fold it up
& toss it in a box
      labeled:
      "things to forget"

tuesday after next

this is top speed
maximum explosion
      an allusion
      an intrusion into your soul
what a fool you must be
      to allow yourself to fail
set up to break down
build up to fall

there is a drive in you, boy!
a deep down abyssal desire
      to lunge into the air
      & fly through hoops of fire
run razors on your skin
and turn your back on all your friends

run away you weak fiend
go back to what you were
do you remember?
how easy it was to fuck & flee?
      hit it & quit it?
      nail it & bail it?
      hump it & dump it?
      fuck it & chuck it?
you can be that again

rip out your heart!
tear it to even more shreds
make sure to connect eyes with your victims
as you destroy the innocence
      in their heads

everything goes round & round
      begins & begins again
everything runs in circles
      there goes the calliope
      to crash again
(remember how we've
      alluded to this before?)

you are destined to drown in your past
      & live with the mistakes you've made

but now it's even worse
you're so fucked-up
        you will now burn
for all of the good things too

you've been down this road before
        back when
            <u>understanding thursday</u>
            came rapping at your door

midnight has come & gone

awake
       in bed
thinking about you
but looking at a picture
       of the girl i was with before you

i see her & i at a dance
       posing for overpriced pictures
when i try to remember it vividly
       i can't
can't remember even being there
all i have is this 3" x 4" pic
       to prove it ever happened

when i lost that girl
i fell so far
       & felt so goddamned hurt
this was fall 2001
now it's spring 2004
       & i look at her
       & feel nothing

i don't remember what her hair smelled like
i can't remember the feel of her kiss
all i know is that i don't know
       anything about what it used to be like

so i'm up with you in my head
wondering if in three years
       i'll look at a picture of you
       & feel nothing

as i lie here in bed
i am wishing for the pain to stop
i'd give so much for it to go away
although, truthfully
i'd rather wish for you
       lying here beside me
the scent of your hair in my nostrils
       & the feel of your kiss
       on my lips

_____ **cool as shit**
 (& shit's pretty cool)

i have a vial of liquid forever
 in my pocket
a gram of infinity's power in my locket
wanna drop a drip?
 & tip a sip?
moisten our lips
 & take off like a rocket?

stories for once upon ...
(or "english shit-erature")

in my freshmen english class
i wrote short stories that had profane words
    & my teacher said i couldn't do that
we watched Hitchcock's 'Rebecca'
    & as a creative writing assignment
    we had to write a new ending
mine included t-rexs with bandanas,
    afros, nazi smurfs
    & a large explosion
my teacher said she wouldn't accept it

we did a section on mythology
    & we all had to write reports
    on mythological figures
mine was prometheus
this assignment was mandatory to pass
no matter what grade i had
    if i didn't do this i'd fail
so i wrote it last minute & it went like this:
    prometheus was a man
    who created fire,
    every day a vulture
    would eat his liver,
    but luckily it grew back
and passed the class i did

in sophomore english class
all i remember doing is reading <u>antigone</u>
besides that all i recall
    is flunking the entire 2nd semester
    & going to summer school
    for 3 weeks

in summer school that year
    our teacher was new & cool
we'd go to the park for two hours every morning,
    this is where i wrote my first poems
    and i remember being shocked
    at how good they were
    but threw them away

every friday we'd watch movies
we watched 'The Goonies', something else
    & the almighty 'Halloween'
i wrote a report on Anthony Burgess
talking about
    A Clockwork Orange
    & The Wanting Seed

in junior english class
we read The Great Gatsby
    & i stole my copy of the book
i still have it
    (later found out Tim did the same thing)
i flunked the entire year this time
    & back to summer school i came

in summer school that year i went for 6 weeks
we watched 'Red Dawn', 'Apocalypse Now'
    & read a lot about war
this is where & when i wrote my
    "amateur trilogy"
"hypothyrca", "rimbaudous importante"
    & "atrocity exhibition"
the teacher was hot

in senior year we read
    'The Canterbury Tales' & 'Beowulf'
& i would sit there and dig
    my nails into my legs
wanting to scream & throw my textbook
    out the window
one day we had to do a big group project
i was standing at my locker
    which is right outside that class
people in my group walked by and said "hi"
i closed my locker door
    & walked five miles home
    for no reason
this was on my 18th birthday

a week later the teacher
    who was known as the nicest guy
told me to get out of his class

i was the first person he had ever kicked out
    & that makes me
    oh so fucking proud
he said i could come back 2nd semester
    but i refused

so 6 more weeks of summer school
even after graduating & walking
    across the stage
this time we read <u>Frankenstein,</u>
    <u>1984,</u> & <u>Brave New World</u>
& we had to write a paper
    compare, contrast
    or compare & contrast
so i wrote a paper
    comparing <u>1984</u> & <u>Brave New World</u>
basing the paper on how much i hated both
i would question the teacher & talk out
    & act up
i think she was afraid of me
so i flunked 2 and a half years
    of english
& i was first published at 21
    of course it doesn't mean my shit is good
or that i know anything about grammar
    or punctuation
but at least i had a little fun

20d

on his way to the health clinic
a car crash decapitated him
had he made it to his destination
he would have found out he was HIV positive
i guess god is gentle sometimes

i love(d) being able to say "we"

choking on the wires
    your lies are hanging on
that dreaded sun is dead and gone
my streamlined face still can't stand
your winded breath of deceit
caught up on the airfoil limbs of this body
these eclectic diversions of yours
    destined & designed
to destroy & turn to rubble
    all of what we had
    this time

diverse perversity
    (or "sodomy in the 6" degree")

tonight after your placation
    & the quickness of
    jumping into bed
i'm going to find out
    all of the secrets
    in your head
for my phallus is hypodermic
    & my semen sodium pentathol
i will inject you
    & you will confess your sins

diary of a sad man
(or "when the ink on the quill runs dry")

wisdom ruptures
       like teeth through my skull
in a hole i dug again
must descend
       & amend
these splitting seams
       while the pieces
       of destroyed dreams
       flutter about

seeing through the morning fog
       & dying trees
a path through this forest
       with broken limbs
       & fallen leaves
i walked into my past once again
seeing that dirty whore in the mirror
       my face old & wrinkled
too much for this young man
i don't want to go through this again

the air i breath is a chemical powder
       struggling mind over matter
branches & thorns
       tear my clothes to tatters
splatters of blood across my face
       & skin
all of it begins
       & i don't want
       to go through this again

cubs in the lion's den

all the cryin' children take my hand
as the bullets fly through this wasteland

book-bags dropping, sprinklers raining,
    & lockers explode
children dying, cameras filming,
    & the TV rights are sold

in this institution where everything is unlearned
the patients, are the students,
    are the victims
pipe bombs go off to singe teenage skin
    & burn

no prom this year
just a new-born dance of fear
tomorrow there'll be metal detectors
    & s.w.a.t. members near
to teach & instill the mentality
death for fame is a commodity
    & that in this real reality
only through violence
    will the deaf ears hear

all the crying children take my hand
    (let's try)
as the bullets fly through this wasteland
    (we'll die)
all the crying children take my hand
    (to heaven our souls we'll send)
as bullets fly through this wasteland
    (we face our present end)

innocence dies in seconds
    without a second of hesitance
& all we have on the plates to blame
    are the hardworking, apathetic parents

our children & future murdered in a day
sucked up, covered over, & swept away

five years ago the perception of teens changed

five years from now i promise
        a new tragedy will make the last
        look like chump-change

playground compounds & lunch-line processions
choirs on the raisers
        singing requiems for the freshmen
letter jackets rebuilt with flack
lackadaisical attitudes
        replaced by paranoia
        of a two man (three?)
        black trench-coat attack

adolescence is all but gone
pubescent exploration is a thing of the past
all you have is guerilla warfare in the study halls
& code-red drills, with fire blankets on the walls

perverse diversity

peripatetic evangelism
        a corporation that is deemed to dwell
barbiturate & kinetic alcoholism
        is sent down to that darling hell

(none of this makes sense so bear with me)

bleeding spleen splitting my sides
fluorescein illuminating my eyes
there flies the ubiquitous eagle
        with atrophied wings
        & those staccato cries

bleat the beats of bilingual terrorists
with bile-stained fists
        & filibustering scrappy fisticuffs
stone-cold frozen faces
lying to rose-cheek bluffs

bluffs so high & melancholy
if you spit it'll drain you dry

masterful teachings by an underdog
        hogging all the truth
goth & mystic delusion
        allude to starving raving youth

a spring board dive into a pool without any water

like a rotary engine
        i have a three-chambered heart
it's all there for your pleasure
        to rip & tear part
your allegorical rhetoric
        & diarist-fake loquaciousness
is all a front for your ...

surreptitious, delectable, & atomic fire balls

the pug-nosed bitch
        with the droopy tits
wants to sample my taste
so i say "fuck it"
        take it out for her to suck it
it's only my life i'll waste

hi-fives in a coffeehouse

is it time for another poem of hope?
about a heartbroken man learning to cope?
washing away his dirty past with antibacterial soap?
yeah, maybe, probably, but truthfully, nope!

only when i look down at the
        black lines on this almond page
does the pain in my head no longer rage
visions of the girl i loved
        even with her statutory age
all those times with her unfold
        as glorious images
        in a sparkling,
        poetic masquerade

united rape of america
(or "suck my dictatorship")

pitchforks & bricks
       in high-flying fists
       in the air
golden sun baking the ground
a million men, women, & children
       protest, riot
screaming, yells & sounds
       down the streets of d.c.
in the mall, battalions of families
       gather rounds
politicians held up in the capitol
       stuffing notes & bills
       into suitcases
not looking out the five-story window
not gazing down at the bloated red faces

there was a rebirth of consciousness
a new age of enlightenment
like a virus it spread from house to house
       from anuses to mouths
the citizens all infected
       with this disease called
       "thinking for yourselves"
they all stopped to finally inhale
they looked around and saw a world
       outside their door
reachable & attainable
they glared at the glowing boxes
       in their living rooms
a contained cancer called TV

people stopped and tasted the food they ate
       feces in the form
       of microwavable stupidity
bite size bits of apathy
mouthfuls of control

with these new eyes they saw
       that this country is a rapist
       fucking the asshole of the world

that this so-called government are pedophiles
  dangling candy out the windows
  of their limos
seeing that church & state
  are a married gay couple
  in bed together every night
but telling us through fake media
  that homosexuality isn't right
that foreigners are stealing jobs
  & darkies are thieving slobs

we've been chugging these lies for years
struggling to immunize our kids
while politicians pillage & take
  & get filthy fucking rich
using a terrorist attack as an excuse
  to blow up iraq
so we can have all the oil
  & the politicians frat buddies'
  companies can get the bid
  to rebuild all we killed

the orphanage that was bombed
  with children's brains painting walls
will soon be a burger playground
either burger queen or mcdonnell's

civilians lined up in rows
  battalions & squads & ranks
staring down national guard tanks
no longer will we be a nation of fools
as we massacre the senators
  piles of bodies
  filling reflecting pools

this corruption has gone on too long
no new world order will we let them make
all of this will be cleaned up
  and we will start again
once a president's head
  is on a fucking stake

in the pages hot off the press

oh, ho, hum!
on the sand-niggers
       we'll drop another bomb!
oh, boy what a thrill!
a toothless shoeless
       girl we'll kill!
firebombing crowded streets
napalming parks & fields
bullets in the brains
       of these brown starving savages
       after we slice & dice their heels

here is $100,000 for a humvee
       & $69.50 for a month of TV
show me the blood & gore
       my taxes pay for
but oh my god!
       a woman's breast on TV!
this country has been disgraced!!

a few words for kelly on a thursday night

i know a single kiss from you
       can make this all go away
but that is far from happening
       still i look forward to that day

quotidian tearjerker: part two

she missed two periods in a row
she knew something wasn't right
buying a pregnancy test
    & confirming its results
      with a trip to the clinic
she was in fact pregnant
    3 months in

she told her parents
    who cursed her
her father slapped her across the face
"not my daughter! not my daughter!
    get the fuck out my house!!"
she is only 16
she grabbed her things & then ran out the door
not ever wanting to look back

she only has 6 months
time is catching up to her
she knows she needs a place to stay

there was one guy
a friend from the past who would help her
he has been in love with her for years
with tears in her eyes she knocks on his door
he opens it to see her saddened face
he then opens his arms & welcomes her

he is 19, they met in drama class
    his junior year
he is well-off & very giving
"of course you can stay here"

she explained it all
    about the baby
    her parents
& he was the first to know
    about the rape
he once knew the guy who did it
    & knew he was a fucking snake

she felt bad to use this guy

                for his generosity
but what else could she do
he too was lonely & needed someone
            & one plus one equals two
she kept her job at the paint store
            to help pay her share
saving as much as she could
            to start her life anew

he would come home from work
            & hear her crying
            & throwing up in the bathroom
holding flowers & a teddy bear
months past & they grew closer
becoming the best of friends
then on june 12th
            her water broke
& they were never the same again

he rushed her to the hospital
            & into the delivery room
he was beside her the whole time
            during her 10-hour labor
just like he was there for her
            for the lamaze classes
every tuesday
            & thursday night
he was there
through it all
            the contractions
            placenta flying
            & the pain
it ended at 12:03 a.m.
when the first screams
            of the newborn were heard
she looked up through tired eyes
            sweat pouring over her
            & her body aching
            & saw him crying
her best friend
            & in this instant
she knew he was a father
maybe not biologically

            but he was truly a friend
            & a real man

they put the young daughter
            in the new mother's arms
            for the first time
& he sat beside her in the bed
they named the child charlotte
            & they knew
            this wasn't the end
he had a little box in his pocket
            & in that pocket was a ring
he was scared to rush this all
            it had only been six months
he knew she was still young
            & unsure of life
but he knew that her love for him
            would come
he pulled out the box
            & extended his arm
dropping one knee to the floor
the doctors & nurses
            seeing him before she did
enthralled by the smell
            & feel of her child
            her child
            her child
she then looked over to see
            a diamond ring shining
brighter than the baby's
            newly-seeing eyes
            & he said:
"i know you don't love me
            but you are my best friend
            & your friend i always vow to be
            i want to stand beside you
            through everything you do,
            so mercedes will
            you marry me?"

& she said ...

            ... to be continued ...

head-to-tail euphemisms

am i to be the excess?
        the leftovers?
the cut frames left on the floor?

this is spinning out of control
        tires slipping
        rain-slick road
        pockmarked with potholes

alone & drunk in this car
        no one to help grab the wheel
no matter how destructive this gets
it'd take a lot to make me feel

am i to be the static charge
        on the r-rated film?
to shock the audience
        with this electrified celluloid

i don't care how tragic & graphic
        this all gets
i just want to be
        spliced back into your life

k.m.s.

no one else
    got to see my dark & light sides
    as much as you
no one else
    slept beside me as many nights as you did
no one else
    meant so much to me to make me change
no one else
    showed me what love really is
no one else
    made love to me
    that felt liked it was earned
    & deserved
no one else
    has ever fit the vision of my perfect wife
no one else
    held me so close
    for so long
no one else
    coveted me like you
no one else
    waited so patiently
    with hope in their eyes
no one else
    will ever replace you
no one else
    ever left me when
    i didn't deserve it
no one else
    gave up on me
    like you did

extempore expectoration of the vile yet frugal seed

you can not tell me that
when the planes dive down
    & drop their radioactive payload
    on our streets
you won't look up
    knowing this is the end
    (a nuclear holocaust)
& smile with teary eyes
    to mouth "thank you"

inhalation

while Ferlinghetti hops between the sheets
    feeling for the angel in his bed
i sit crying & writing
    trying to forget
    the angel
    in my head

may 1st, 2004 - saturday

"in the first night
    in which we lose ourselves
    and know each other"*

i could dream a million dreams
    & live a thousand lives
just to fathom all that
    is in the above lines

*("from the 'moving waters' of Gustave Klimt"
    by Lawrence Ferlinghetti)

_____ **lackman estates**

may 1st, 2004
        saturday
        2:22 p.m.
(just like in "This Is Not A Love Song"
        by the The Juliana Theory)

dusted the living room today
        or "undusted" as we say
vacuumed the whole house
sitting on the porch again
        in the green rocking bench swing
        or whatever the fuck it is!
"Division St." is playing

a guy who lives across the street
        and one house over
is out mowing his yard
        his name is Dan
i've lived in this house since 1984
        come december
(if we're still here, it'll be 20 years exactly)
Dan has lived here as long as we have
he has seen my brother & i grow
        from those rambunctious kids
        to those rowdy teens
        to lost men
i have never heard him speak
        nor have i ever said
        a word to him
right across the street
        a new family? couple?
is moving in
this is the 3rd or 4th
        to inhabit that house
i remember crawling on a rock pile
        that used to be the front yard
before the house was even built
for a while it was an empty lot
        with houses all around
back when this was a dead end street
back when the Ferris family were our best friends
"Steps Ascending" is now playing

i remember planting all of the trees
        in our yard
once little saplings
        now trees that tower
        higher than our house
they've grown & spread
        & aged
        like me
i need to leave this place
"War All The Time" is playing now

i'm waiting to see the hot girl
        with the camaro
        come out of her house
she lives in the room where
        Erin & Allison used to live
her basement was where i saw my first naked girl
        (in preschool?!)
her basement is where i saw my first
        hardcore porn
        (in 3rd grade?!)

it's kind of funny to be able to
look at a house and see more history in it
than the people that live there now

i need to leave this place

president john "dubya" quisling

vote for me in '04
    i promise not to lie
vote for me in '04
    i promise to make
    all the dirty jews & camel-fuckers die
vote for me in '04
    i'll sell you all out
    to my old frat buddies & cronies
investing your social security
    into their companies
    & stock market
that way they'll be able to build
    their mansions
    with 54 lavatories!
vote for me in '04
    i'll keep rubbing 9-11 in your face
    & use it as an excuse
    to invade canada
those hockey-playing mother-fuckers have it coming
"why?"
    well they pose a threat
you see they once heard a story about a guy
    whose friend's cousin's sister's
    brother's best friend's boyfriend's
    uncle's neighbor's boss' son's
    friends read a story about a nuclear program
vote for me in '04
    i'll cut medicare
    & all other healthcare programs
i'll cut funding for libraries, schools,
    & the arts
we'll spend $3 trillion a year
    to rebuild montreal
vote for me in '04
    i'll catch bin laden
    & execute him on pay-per-view
but really what i'll do his suck his cock
    flip off the cameras
    & shit on the american flag
while i laugh
    & osama tongues my balls
vote for me in '04

    you know you'll eat it up
    all the mud we rake & serve
vote for me in '04
    & i'll give those
    welfare-collecting single mothers of five
    what those black bitches deserve
vote for me in '04
    i'll allow gay marriages
    but only in certain cities
put all of the fags & dykes together
    & have them register for the holocaust
i mean gay pride parade
as they march in the streets
    waving the grand ol' fag (flag)
on their way to my ovens
vote for me in '04
    i never saw any combat
    & deserted to come home & protest
    throwing my ribbons & medals over the fence
but i'm still the best candidate you're gonna get
    to be commander-in-chief
    of this country's defense
vote for me in '04
    so you'll no longer have to worry
    about free speech anymore
vote for me in '04
    so my storm troopin' s.s. squad
can beat down your fuckin' door!

rallentando

this is for the boy
      who'll never know me
this is for the boy
      who will never hear my voice
this is for the boy
      sitting on his porch
      or in a dark room
      under a lonely light
this is for the boy
      reading the words
      in this book
      long after i am dead
this is for the boy
      who understands all of this
this is for the boy
      i'll never see
this is for the boy
      i'm writing for

i hope you're proud of me

a pole without a flag
(on a day with a rapturous wind)

one of my favorite things
        to do as a child
was to dive into a pool
        sink to the bottom
        & turn around
        lying on my back
staring up at the bodies above me
        the light's rays beating down
all of what i see is rippling
wishing i could hold my breath
        forever
not ever wanting to come up
knowing that when i emerge
i would be a man
with no more
        beautiful rippling images
        to gaze upon

the girl with stars on her hand that she cried from her eyes
sitting on the futon
        where we once slept side-by-side
i look out the window
        into the dark world
        outside these lonely walls
you're out there with someone else
        in your head
        someone else is putting
        a smile on your face
i look & see my reflection in the window
        & i have no smile

_____ pulling your teeth from my bloody knuckles
you don't make a difference
you don't change the world
you don't make them remember you
by becoming
        a member of the crowd
you achieve this all
        by massacring it

_____ so says the children
the last american eagle
        is begging to be shot down
for the america he sees
        is not the one he knows & loves

_____ you're holding on tight to your beliefs of letting me go
you are the rainmaker
        leaving me behind
to drown in my memories
        & tears

_____ the runaway
is it that she loved me?
or loved her boyfriend
        because that is what
        you're supposed to do?

is it that i loved her?
or did i just love my girlfriend
        because that is what
        i was supposed to do?

i am calling out to the girl i love
who has her hands over her ears

answers to questions you'll never ask

shut it out!
shut it out, shut it up!

shut it out!
shut it out!
shut your mind off!

only when i sleep
        do the visions fade
i thank the pills for fighting them off
sweet sweet diphenhyrdamine!!
only when i'm unconscious
        do i not think of her
but when i awake they come back
        to haunt me
torment me & make me hurt

she was my best & closest friend
        for a year
and i can't face her
i want to cut her out completely
but goddamn i love her so

it's only been a week
        & i'm tired of thinking
        & tired of writing about it all

"every line is about who i don't wanna
        write about anymore"

the breakup songs
        make sense again
& in the end
        i'll never win

i'm tired of losing friends
i'm tired of loves at ends

i want to turn this all off
i want to turn this all away
i just wanna breathe deep
        & not choke on

    the pain in my chest
i just wanna breathe deep
   & sleep
   & never dream

all those dreams i dreamed of you & me
hurt me now
'cause i'll never see
   your smiling face again

as much as i want to be with you
i know i can't even face you
i've been repeating the same shit
   in different ways
writing about the love i lost
   & all my lonely days

shut it out!
turn it off!
please just begin your fade
it's what you want anyway

cool by association
(or "a resurgence of the bourgeoisie")

xxxiii
lights are turning off
people are turning their backs
i am closing my eyes
not wanting to witness their attacks

xxxiv
the cars are slowing down
bumpers are almost touching
in a hurry to get where we're going
but we stop to see the wreck

xxxv
face me & taste my flesh
guess what tomorrow will bring
just another day without you
& a lifetime with a finger
        without a ring

xxxvi
five o'clock shadow
i don't know, i don't know
trembling fingers & quivering lips
necks snapping to see twisting hips

xxxvii
see it all fall
and rise again to fly away
so smile & cry at the same time
to a sentence full of
        words that'll never rhyme

quotidian tearjerker: part three

she still cried every once in a while
    about what he did
    & all she has been through
but everything began to fade away
her parents came to visit her
    & their grandchild
    sweet charlotte
& begged for forgiveness
    & it was given
one day she woke up
    & realized that
she is, was, and always will be
    better than the guy who raped her
she feels so stupid now
to have thought that any of it
    was her fault
    he was the terrible person
her husband
    & best friend, tim
would hold her & kiss her
    all those weeping nights
they never consummated their marriage
    until their two-year anniversary
she was 18 & finally comfortable
    enough to let a person
    touch her again
they made sweet, gentle love
    keeping quiet
so they could hear their child
    in case she needed anything
she did see the guy who hurt her once more
walking down the street outside of
    the paint store
    she is now the manager of
he looked into the window
    saw her
    & his eyes fell
    to the ground
he was so ashamed to see her
    knowing what he did

three weeks later he was killed

when a car crossed the center lane
    & hit him head-on
she heard about this
    and did feel bad for him
    but had no more tears to cry
she is a mother
    & a wonderful one at that
she is a wife
    & a beautiful one, no less
her husband is the greatest
    person she has ever known
& her daughter
    is the most amazing
    of all those precious stones

she was the victim of a rape
    a dark & disgusting act
& that day a seed of deceit
    was planted
but no matter how deep
    you plant a seed
it will always grow up & out
    to face the shining sun
& will blossom to be
    a gorgeous woman
    & extraordinary person

in the end
she made it through

confession

this book is almost over. i am surprised by how quick i filled this fuckin' thing. <u>understanding thursday</u> was a damn 6x9 sketchbook without any lines. and writing as big and sloppy as i do it still took me almost two years to finish it. but this book which is about 230 pages (that's front & back) and having 29 college-ruled lines per page, i still filled it in less than a year.

written in the bottom corner of every page is a page number, all odd numbers written on every other page. back on february 2nd, 2004 the page number was 45. which means that from september 18th, 2003 to february 2nd, 2004 i had only hand-written 45 pages. but now i am on page 202. meaning that from february 2nd, 2004 - may 3rd, 2004 i have hand-written 157 pages. going to the coffeehouse a lot (and becoming a stereotype) helped & unfortunately so did losing kelly.

(sighs)

i wouldn't have minded this book taking me five years to write as long as Kelly was still by my side. but sometimes you have to stop dreaming.

when i began this journey i knew where the finish line was but couldn't see it. so i began slow & paced myself. covering every mile & giving each piece the thought it deserved. (kind of, not really) but when i caught a glimpse of the finish line i just went crazy & burned through all of the energy i had. so now i am mere steps from splitting the tape with my chest, but i barely have the will to do so. i have been rewriting the same bullshit for the last three months. not really putting forth that much effort. and i'm not talented enough to write anything really spectacular to conclude this all. and i'm too lazy to go back and redo all of the horrid pieces.

i still believe poems are for the minutes in which they are written.

this all is concluding & growing weak, but that is how i feel right now.

i know that in less than a month i'll be engrossed in my next book. book 4. and not care much about this one. my works will begin to change & hopefully they will get better.

this is the final part in my "growing up" trilogy. the work i do from now on i am going to try & make a little different. perhaps i'll sell out & start writing poems about trees & gardens, & drinking wine with my bourgeois friends.

i doubt it too.

it has been six years, 396+ poems, many dark nights, a few broken hearts (mine and others') and i'm still here.

i'm sorry if i've disappointed you in any way. but please come back for more.

from now on the fucking gloves are off, bitches!

and there is no mother-fucking holding back!

more gibberish

could you imagine
        what it would be like
        if men could ejaculate diamonds?
think of all of the women lined up on their knees
(i apologize for the objectification, but not really)
then again if every guy could do that
        then diamonds wouldn't be so rare

or what if semen tasted like
        chocolate-chip cookie-dough ice cream?
man, that'd be crazy!

(yeah, i don't know what goes through
        my head either)

two-year anniversary
(or "the last words")

on this day in 2002 my ex-girlfriend
       began to date my best friend
       & the pain i felt was great
now on this day 2004 i said these words
       to the girl i loved
       more than anyone
       & was my best friend for over a year

Brett: did you love me?
Kelly: yes
Brett: were you my friend?
Kelly: yes
Brett: then listen to me, are you listening?
Kelly: yes
Brett: this will be the last thing i ever say to you.
      i will never call you again, or e-mail you,
      or pass words through someone else.
      this is the last thing i am ever gonna say
           (sighs, cries, breathes)
      i loved you more than anyone in my life.
      you were one of the greatest people i
      have ever known. but you have hurt me
      & instilled more pain in me than anyone else
      & i hate you for that. but not really.
      i love you so much, but fuck you,
      & fuck what we had. goddamn it, Kelly.
      i love you so much but fuck you.

long way down *
    (one last thing)

movies never change, their images
    always stay the same
although the actors, & actresses
    grow old & die

books never change, their words & ink
    stay the same
although the authors may change & adapt
    & their newer work may be different

music will never change, the CDs will
    stay the same
the vocals, guitars & drums will always
    remain the way they are on a record
although the artists may die
    or bands break up

all of these things will stay the same
    no matter how old you get

every book, movie, & cd i have
    will live longer than me
    & never change

i adore these things because they'll
    never grow away from me,
    tell me they love me
    & then leave me

the crossroads

i have a warped mind
        a corrupted mind
        & it has been like that
        for years
always looking further & deeper
i don't know why

there is this moment i remember
        from elementary school
i think it was 4th grade
i was sitting on the ground, outside
        during recess
kids were playing kickball, four square
        & swinging
i was sitting under this overhang
it was winter because everyone
        had on heavy coats

i was watching this girl
        a girl talking to other girls
i had a huge & embarrassing crush on her
her name was Sarah
she knew i liked her because i always told her
        & had everyone else in the school
        tell her as well

i looked at her & i thought
we're all going to grow up
i saw her & these girls
        & knew soon they would be growing breasts
        & having their periods
we were all 10 or 11 so i don't know
        if girls were to that point yet or not
i saw these girls & envisioned
        and not in a sexual fantasy way
that someday soon they'll be touched
        & lose their virginity
they'd be getting married
        & having babies
they'd become drunk sorority girls
        & do disastrous things
they'd grow up

  & forget their innocence
& of course boys would grow too
  along with these girls
becoming the guys that touched the girls
  & knocked them up

we all were just kids
  with breath steaming in the cold
  playing during recess
for some reason i was a 4th-grade kid
seeing all of the things to come

i am now 22 & passed all
  of the things i foresaw
i was looking ahead but not far enough
  to see me
  sitting alone
looking back at the 4th-grade me
wanting to do it all over
  but this time
  do it right

paroxysm

a tiny moment
        you remember forever
a simple moment
        of beauty
a hand running over a lover's stomach
        & slowly a finger runs under
        the waistline of clothing
the lover sucks in their little belly
        an inaudible submission
        a silent "yes"

shitwanga

will we ever turn our eyes away?
will we ever see the trees?
will we ever look past
        the flashing lights
        & busted fenders
to see the fields of flowers beyond?

the final countdown
(we're almost there)

i have come full circle
i am alone once more
feeling the pain of losing love
it has been two years
      & i feel the same
but
      i am not the same

i have grown
i have changed
i write as often as i have always wanted
i think harder & longer
      about my choices than before
i am smarter
i am wiser
i know where this path leads
      & i am aware of how i once was
      & what i did
now that i am here again
i won't make the same mistakes

i am not happy
i see the world around me
      & am aware of the changes to come
i am not happy
i am lonely
      & i just want to love
      & be loved
but there is no one to love me
and even if i find someone
would my past scare them away too?

i am lonely
      & hurt
i just want to love
but for now
i want to destroy
      & cause pain
i know the right path to walk
      & part of me

            doesn't want to
part of me just wants
            to run myself into the ground
            like i did years ago
do you know why?

because fuck you!

that's why

no man of woman born
(the story of the bracelet)

san diego, ca
june 1998
a marine corps or naval base
    (i forget which one)
on coronado island
    (where they filmed 'the stuntman')
i found a silver-ball chain
    like the kind dog-tags
    are connected to
i put it in my bag
    & took it home with me

since freshman or maybe sophomore year
    Kirk had this black leather rope
    wrapped around his right wrist
it was on there for years
    & i always wanted something like that

june 17th, 1998
i cut the bracelet down
    & wrapped it twice around my right wrist
i remember going to work to pick up my check
that night a girl i knew from work
    & who i was kind of seeing
    came over to my house,
    her name was Mandy
we watched 'The Goonies'
    & as the credits rolled
we both got naked
    & i gave her my virginity
i remember being in the push-up position
    with her body under mine
    & seeing the chain on my wrist

driving her home later
    i listened to "kasjmir"
    & tossed the used condom
    on the street behind Tim's house
    (i still have the wrapper)
all of this was three years before i ever met Kelly

but june 17th, 1998 was her 12th birthday

september 13th, 1999 i began to date
        another girl, named Marilyn
by this time i put a black rope on my wrist
        & so did she
        to symbolize our love
both of them kept falling off & breaking
        & we had to repeatedly fix them
(a perfect analogy for our relationship)

in the year & a half since losing my virginity
        i slept with 7 girls
five one time each
one about six times
        & the other a lot more than that

Marilyn & i dated for two years
        & two weeks
bringing us to october 2001
by this time my number was 10
Kelly & i first slept together
        september 1st, 2001

an interesting side story to all of this
is when visiting Marilyn at college
        in january of 2002
i recognized a girl in a picture of
        Marilyn's sorority
the girl i recognized Marilyn
        had talked to once or twice about me
it was Mandy

by summer of 2002
        my number was 12

i will admit that when i was younger
i thought the bigger the number
the better the man
i was stupid but what can i say
i thought it would make me a man
but i think now
looking back and realizing this

        doesn't make you a man
        actually makes you a man

so throughout this all
        i still had this damned bracelet
        on my right wrist
it was a symbol of me
all main characters i wrote in my screenplays
        & various stories
        always had one
& a kanga and roo doll i gave Marilyn
        one christmas
both kanga and roo had little bracelets

anyway
come one day i jumped out of bed
        & big spiggity bam!
it fell off
right to the floor
i went to school
        came back
& took a picture of where it was lying
i then hung the bracelet on the wall
        where it still resides
it falling off ended a long
        & arduous period of my life

it fell off on september 13th, 2002
what would've been my & Marilyn's
        three-year anniversary
that night was the night at penguin park
where & exactly when i knew
        i was truly in love with Kelly

the bracelet was on my wrist for 4 years & 3 months
        or 1,549 days
thus the basis for the title
        of the final piece in
        <u>understanding thursday</u>

within these 1,549 days
        i had sex with 12 girls
i'm not ashamed but i'm not proud

i did many terrible things
    & was a complete bastard
    to a lot of people

but since the bracelet fell off
i have only been with one girl
i have only loved one girl
i have done my best to be a man since then
    & i think i've come through a little

in august of 2003 i put a new bracelet
    on my wrist
    & around march of 2004
    i put a black leather rope
    on my left wrist
(the rope came from a journal Marilyn once
    gave me called a mad jack's fleeting glimpse)

i don't know what these new bracelets mean
    yet
but when i figure them out
    i'll let you know

double crown

a head full of voices
a mouth full of degradation
his eyes blink
        to the ticking of all clocks
the sands of time melt into glass
        to encase his past
        of lies & mistakes
with no salvation in sight

bourgeoisie

xxxviii
love is a fluid
passed intravenously
flowing from you to me
i want all you have to give
for me to live
i will suck you dry

xxxix
dacryphilia lovers
licking liquids from each other's face
'dark side of the moon' revolving
diamond etching, scratching
    & speakers speaking
black light shining down
    glowing smiles
    with tears on their tongues

xxxx
closing my eyes
i see nothing
speaking only to breathe
laughing as a front
to cover the crying
dreaming of a world that's nonexistent
covering my ears
    to drown out
the screaming voices
cackling & begging for me

k.h.b.s.w.t.g.

i finally feel content with my body
    &mind contained within
i actually feel at home in my skin
it's just everywhere else i
    am having a problem with

i don't know the walls
    that are my room
i don't know the neighbors
    in my 'hood
it feels like i don't know
    the people i call my friends
& sometimes i don't even know
    if i want to know them anymore
i love them & care about them
    but i am no longer comforted by them
trying to involve myself in their lives
    takes so much effort
    & rarely do they make an attempt
    to be in mine

i am a page and a quarter page
    from filling this book
(i already wrote the final piece,
    i never actually hand wrote
    it in here)

i am for the first time happy with myself
i am for the first time at home inside my skin
but now that i have transcended all
    & become what i have always
    wanted to become
now that i am full of love
    & friendship
    & no longer want to hurt anyone
i look around to see
there is no one to be proud of me
there is no one who knows this new
    & true
    me
is this what they call irony?
is this some kind of cosmic joke?

i guess so
maybe i'll find it funny someday
yeah maybe
playing   yeah   playing
i was a child then ...

      'til the stree—

oh, wait we've already done this!

i was a child
now i am a man
alone to fight through this life
i'm ready but just have one last task

enjoy my last

obloquy
(or "the trilogy comes to an end")

yesterday is lying on the floor
    throat slit
    & gasping for poisoned air
tomorrow runs screaming out the door

our man tuesday stands
    chest filling & emptying
    temper rising to never fall
he has a dagger in his bloody hands
    & carmine eyes
flames shoot out his nose
    & smoke billows out
    of his mouth

there is no reason
    no control in his mind
just chaotic rage
    <u>understanding</u> is dead & gone

he screams & it shatters
    his crystal goblets
    & glass mug
he picks up his stool from his desk
    & throw is it into
    his shelf of CD's
and kicks his foot through the window

slamming his fists into his posters
    & concert-ticket covered walls
throws his 'Halloween' collection to the floor
unzips his pants & pulls out his tiny cock
    pissing all over
knocks his screenplays from the shelves
    tearing the pages
tossing them & all of his books
    (read & unread)
    into a pile
takes the knife & slashes through
    his photo albums
slicing the emulsion & paper throats

                    of his friends
he takes a machete to his DVD's
            & VHS cassettes
destroys his posters, buttons,
            & childhood art projects
(all art created merely for the sake of it)

he screams again
            but this time it is silent
but the inaudible sound waves
            cause ripples in the confetti
            of torn pages
            filling the room

he takes a bottle of whiskey
            gulps down a large swig
and he spins arms outstretched
            like a sprinkler
            he sprays the walls
            & floors
yearbooks & his new bed
            doused in gasoline
soaking all the sheets
ready to fulminate

he is nothing he was
he is everything he is destroying
dying to be reborn
lighting a match
            with the fire of his breath
tossing it into the kindling
            (love letters from all those girls)
it takes light

he rips off his black bracelet
            on his left wrist
but leaves the silver one
            on his right
a small token
a reminder
            of what he is killing today
digs his nails into the fabric
            of his clothing

tearing them from his body
shredding them
    & scarring himself
his clothes fuel the burn
    & his dick hangs freely
downs one more swig of whiskey
    & pours the rest over his flaccid cock
disinfecting it
    & erasing its memory
    of the women it has stabbed

he bursts through his front door
    & walks into his yard
sky burning down
the house engulfed in flames
    flames licking the heavens above
machete still in hand
    he skips into the street
    chopping down the streetlights
so they will never come on again

he laughs a crazed laugh
knowing this is the end of the end
    & it will never begin again

the house burns down
    as his cock goes erect
he strolls into this new world
    after killing what & who he was

walking out into this world
with one final primal scream
    & his fist
    raised in the air

2018 Notes

In the movie world, *'til the streetlights came on* and *understanding thursday* could arguably be seen as the low-budget indie flicks that I directed, before getting my first major-studio release *ars gratia artis*.

    ars gratia artis is the first book of poetry that I had written, that really had a beginning and ending in mind. It was also the first time that I had real time to focus on writing; and a place to focus that writing. I didn't have a relationship to distract me; and my job had changed, so I wasn't as distracted by that either. My world changed from the Regal Crew to the B.N.S.F. world. I spent a lot of time alone, and didn't spend too much time with friends. My world started to revolve around Black Dog Coffeehouse; going there to write almost nightly. And this was in the days before I knew anyone there. So to avoid the appearance of "wanting to be seen writing" there, I kept my head down and wrote the fuck outta that place.

ars gratia artis is still one of my favorite books. It is the first time I felt I really had a voice, and had firm legs to stand on. Time has lessened my love for this book, a little; but overall I owe it a lot. It's still rough, but in a good way. I think it was during this book that I tried harder to write better, as opposed to just try harder to be more clever. I wrote darker and more graphic than in *understanding thursday*, but the voice was smoother, so *ars gratia* artis has a much better flow.

ars gratia artis is the end of a three-part trilogy of books. And within that trilogy I feel is encapsulated the greatest progression of style and maturity. After *ars gratia artis* it becomes relatively routine. There is very little change in style from *ars gratia artis* to the end of this series: *reality vs. perception*.

Love your faces.

the*BAC*
2018
West Plaza
Kansas City, Missouri

Series One *(1998 to 2006)*
'til the streetlights came on
understanding thursday
ars gratia artis
... for the minutes ...
in lucem proferre ...
... de nocte
x-rated
corruptio optimi pessima
reality vs. perception

Series Two *(2007)*
White Lies & the Confusion of Day Dreams
Black Truth & the Comprehension of Nightmares
Gray Days & the Possibility of Loveless Eyes
Golden Dust & the Resurgence of Youthful Trysts
Magenta Scars & the Delusions of Erudite Whores
Violet Dust & the Detriment of Broken Homes
Green Dreams & the Overflow of Orchidaceous Nights
Silver Rays & the Revolution of Dystopic Cliques
Cyan Lines & the Metamorphosis of Cyclical Tales

Series Three *(2008 to 2012)*
Junkyard Robot
In A World Of Reverse
A Treatise On Repose ...
See The Whole Board
Hums In Hollow Heads
270 Days Later
402 Roosevelt
24 Highway
10-14

Collections - Selected Works
iJihad
iKnew
iZobot
iFade

Collections - Complete Works
3,002 Days
Of An Example Made
Mind Shards
Fiber Scars

ISBN 979-8-89379-377-2

www.ingramcontent.com/pod-product-compliance
Lightning Source LLC
Chambersburg PA
CBHW071436150426
43191CB00008B/1146